50 Gems

of

Northamptonshire

WILL ADAMS

AMBERLEY

Acknowledgements

Many people have helped with the preparation of this book, but I would like especially to thank the following: Katie Burnett at Silverstone Circuit; Mick Coggins of Rothwell Ossuary; Harriet Addy and Carla Cooper of Sulgrave Manor; Jane Baile FSA of Nassington Prebendal Manor; Sue Brown, Administrator at Deene Park; Adele Curtis, Marketing Manager at Northampton Theatres Trust; Henry and Nova Guest at Ashby St Ledgers; the staff at Harrington Aviation Museum; Sarah Harvey at Althorp; Liz Jansson at No. 78 Derngate; Jenny Matts at Holdenby House and Maria Smith at Only Beattie for the picture of Boughton House.

Unless otherwise credited, all the photographs were taken by the author in the summer of 2017.

First published 2017

Amberley Publishing
The Hill, Stroud
Gloucestershire, GL5 4EP

www.amberley-books.com

Copyright © Will Adams, 2017

Map contains Ordnance Survey data © Crown copyright and database right [2017]

Back cover image © Althorp Collection

The right of Will Adams to be identified as the Author
of this work has been asserted in accordance with the
Copyrights, Designs and Patents Act 1988.

British Library Cataloguing in Publication Data.
A catalogue record for this book is available from the British Library.

ISBN 978 1 4456 7438 4 (print)
ISBN 978 1 4456 7439 1 (ebook)

Map illustration by User Design, Illustration and Typesetting.

Origination by Amberley Publishing.

Printed in Great Britain.

Contents

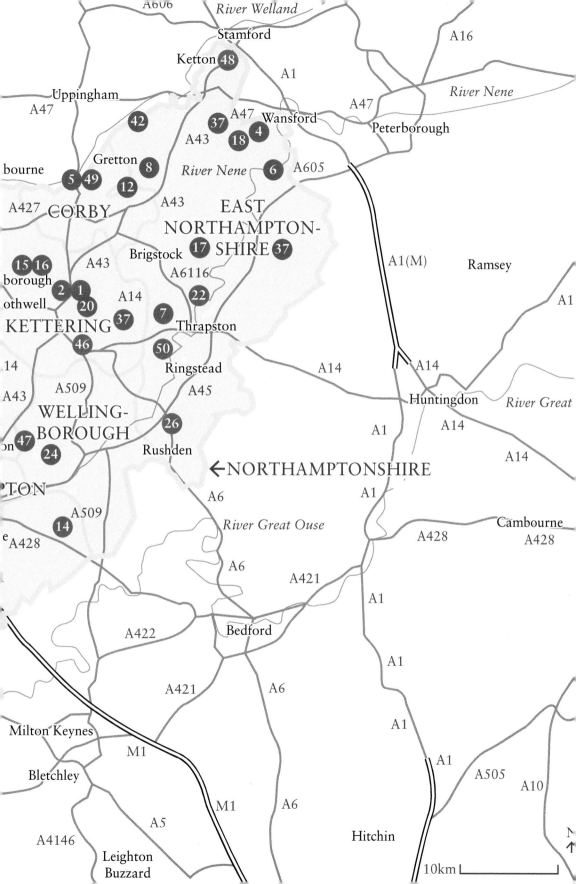

Introduction

Traditionally Northamptonshire has a reputation of being a county that one passes through rather than visits, which is perhaps understandable as it stretches diagonally across England for almost 60 miles from the south-west near Banbury in Oxfordshire to the north-east near Stamford in Lincolnshire. (The county boundary between Northamptonshire and Lincolnshire is the shortest in England, at 19 metres [62 feet]!) It is therefore inevitably crossed by major trunk roads and motorways as well as important north–south rail routes. A line of limestone hills forms the county's backbone, forming the watershed between the Severn basin and The Wash; it was said that 'not a single brook, however insignificant, flows into it from any other district', but only outwards east and west to the sea.

But anyone who does stop to linger will find a county of great beauty and great contrasts. Road signs announce it as the 'Rose of the Shires', but it was also known as the 'county of spires and squires'. Being largely rural, there are countless picturesque villages and country churches – every one of which would qualify as a 'gem' in its own right – and numerous country houses; indeed, the county claims to have more than any other.

Industry is largely concentrated around the larger towns of Northampton, Kettering, Corby, Wellingborough, Rushden, Daventry and Brackley. Boots and shoes were once the most famous product, and small specialist firms still survive. Ironstone quarrying and the iron and steel industry was also important in years gone by, especially around Corby. The disfiguring quarries have since either returned to the landscape or become interesting country parks as at Irchester and at Twywell Hills and Dales, both of which narrowly 'missed the cut' for this book. Gravel extraction along the Nene Valley also left a legacy of pits that have been transformed into a long series of lakes and fisheries – unnatural features, perhaps, but a fine use of ravaged land for leisure and nature.

So whittling down the choice to just fifty 'gems' was a difficult task, and anyone who knows Northamptonshire will be wailing that such-and-such a location has been unjustifiably omitted! What I have tried to do is to include places that are publicly accessible, either for free or on payment of an entry fee. Thus they can all be visited and enjoyed, although these thumbnail portraits only scratch the surface of their rich history and heritage (see their respective websites for more detail).

I was brought up next door in Warwickshire, and Northamptonshire was a foreign land occasionally visited for long-distance picnics. I have now lived here for more than thirty years and am grateful to Amberley Publishing for giving me the opportunity to visit places I've shamefully never seen during that time. I feel I now know the county and its amazing heritage so much better, and hope that you will derive as much pleasure from reading about and visiting Northamptonshire as I have had in researching it. 'Northamptonshire: Britain's Best Surprise!' is the county's current publicity campaign. Prepare to be surprised …

Will Adams, 2017

Historic Structures

1. The Eleanor Crosses: Geddington and Hardingstone

In 1254 the teenage future King Edward I of England and Eleanor, daughter of Ferdinand III of Castile, married. Despite a politically expedient union, it became an unusually close marriage that lasted for thirty-six years. Eleanor was well-loved and popular, and the couple were seldom apart. In 1290 the Queen fell ill on her way to Lincoln, and on 28 November she died at Harby in Nottinghamshire at the age of forty-six.

Her embalmed body was taken south, accompanied by her husband, and at each nightly resting place he ordered that a lavishly decorated stone cross be erected to mark the passing of the cortege. As a result, between 1291 and 1294 a dozen monuments were built, no two alike, but today only three survive more or less intact, two of them in Northamptonshire.

Queen Eleanor's body rested at Geddington on the night of 6/7 December, and the cross erected there in about 1294 is the most modest but the best preserved, despite some repairs and alteration over the centuries. It is the only one of the three to be of triangular section, and is taller and slimmer, standing almost 13 metres high. It was built of local limestone and bears six carved shields, including the arms of England and Castile, while three niches each contain a statue of the Queen.

The cross is also unusual in that it incorporates at its base a conduit house, built in 1769, in which water was collected in cisterns.

The procession's next stop was at Hardingstone, just south of Northampton town centre near Delapre Abbey, where the Queen's body lay. The cross here was begun in 1291, and is octagonal and built in three tiers; as at Geddington, the original lofty cross that topped it has been lost; today's broken shaft is the result of restoration in 1840. The cross was originally completely painted, and the bottom tier includes open books, which may once have carried painted inscriptions of the Queen's life, so that prayers for her soul could be offered by passers-by.

The Geddington cross stands in the middle of a quiet village, and its Northampton counterpart beside the roaring traffic of the A45/A508 junction, but they both speak across seven centuries of a dearly loved Queen and her heartbroken King.

The third surviving cross is at Waltham Cross, Hertfordshire, while the last resting place of the funeral procession was marked by London's Charing Cross.

The Eleanor Cross in the centre of Geddington, with the conduit house below.

The Northampton Eleanor Cross beside the busy A508 near Delapre Abbey.

2. Newton-in-the-Willows Dovecote

What is said to be the largest dovecote in Britain stands near the village church and hamlet of Newton-in-the-Willows, just west of Geddington village. It is all that remain of a mansion built by the Tresham family, a name that we will meet again several times.

The dovecote, built in about 1600, measures nearly 54 feet by 24 feet, with walls 3 feet thick in places and 20 feet high. It is divided internally into two equal compartments, and each half has a small lantern in the roof with ledges to allow the birds to enter and leave. On the south side are two small high windows and low doorways once closed by 4-inch solid oak doors.

The dovecote was designed to accommodate 1,000 pairs of birds in each half, and the nest holes are arranged in the standard checkerboard pattern. It can be accessed from a path from Dovecote Farm Shop.

When the Treshams built their mansion they enclosed the land, depopulated the village and adopted the village church of St Faith as their own private chapel. Now deconsecrated, it is the home of the Newton Field Centre, providing science, geography, biology and fieldwork opportunities to school groups, families and adults.

The dovecote is claimed to be the largest in Britain.

The area was not always so peaceful, however. In 1607 harvests were poor, the weather bad, common land was enclosed and peasants evicted. Large groups of rebellious country folk gathered and King James I issued a royal proclamation ordering their suppression. In June more than forty people were killed in Newton by an army raised by the staunchly Roman Catholic Tresham family.

The 'Newton Rebels' were led by John Reynolds, calling himself 'Captain Pouch', who claimed that his pouch contained 'that which shall keep you from all harm', but which turned out to be a piece of green cheese. The royal proclamation was read twice, but to no avail, and finally a charge led to the deaths and many prisoners being held in St Faith's Church; the ringleaders were tried, hanged and quartered. At the church today there is a memorial to them.

Other dovecotes are to be found in the county – at Isham, Grendon, Hinwick and Podington, among others – but this is the largest.

The Treshams' estate was sold off before the end of the seventeenth century, and the house eventually demolished – no trace of it or its gardens remains save the dovecote and church.

Inside the dovecote
there are nesting boxes
for 2,000 birds.

Above: A stone slab with the name 'Maurice Tresham' below the family's emblem, a triple trefoil.

Left: An information board outside St Faith's Church commemorating the 'Newton Rebellion' of 1607.

3. Charwelton Packhorse Bridge

Several important rivers rise in the Northamptonshire uplands, including the Warwickshire Avon, the Nene and the Cherwell. The latter is an important tributary of the Thames, and gives its name to the delightful village of Charwelton, south of Daventry on the road to Banbury.

Crossing the river in the village is an ancient packhorse bridge, which probably dates from the fifteenth century (some authorities claim the thirteenth century) – in any event it is probably the oldest bridge in the county. Packhorse bridges were designed to allow horses carrying sidebags or panniers to cross rivers; that at Charwelton is about 4 feet wide between the low kerb-like parapets, and is built of ironstone. It has two pointed stone arches separated by a cutwater on the upstream side, and was Grade II* listed in 1968.

The bridge is now only a footbridge, with the present-day main road beside it. That road is the A361, and possibly deserves its own place as one of the quirkier 'gems' of the county. It has the distinction of being the longest three-digit 'A' road in the UK, running for some 200 miles from the A5 at Kilsby through no fewer than seven counties to the seafront at Ilfracombe in Devon. SABRE, the Society for All British and Irish Road Enthusiasts, describes the A361 as 'a long but essentially local road', pointing out that, other than the north Devon section, the motorist would have very little reason to use it other than as a local link rather than a complete through route.

The packhorse bridge in Charwelton village beside the A361.

The side parapets were kept low so as not to foul the horse's panniers.

SABRE's founder claims that the A361 'is without doubt a blessed road. How could it not be, taking in both Avebury ... and Glastonbury. It is the road to the promised land.' Originally just joining Taunton with Banbury, it was extended to its present extent first in 1935, then again in the 1960s and the 1980s. These extensions 'appear to have been done simply because the A361 was the most suitable number available to signify a major continuous through route', says SABRE, 'yet neither really bears much relation to the course of the rest of the road. One could get the feeling that this is a road that simply doesn't know when to stop.'

Certainly the fifteenth-century packhorses are unlikely to have been heading for Ilfracombe!

Historic Houses and Castles

4. Nassington Prebendal Manor

This Grade I-listed manor dating from about 1230 is the earliest surviving dwelling in Northamptonshire. The site has a history going back to the Anglo-Saxon period; excavations in the 1980s revealed traces of a building from the end of the tenth century.

A Prebendary (from the Latin word for 'pension') was a senior member of the clergy, normally supported by revenues from an estate or parish. In return the office-holders oversaw the churches whose revenues they held. Prebendaries were in effect bishop's deputies, playing a role in the administration of the cathedral, but had a fixed and independent income, making them independent of the bishop. They were often absent – some never even visited Nassington – so a clerk would probably live at the Prebend to deal with any ecclesiastical issues.

King Cnut was an early visitor to Nassington in about 1020, and possibly owned a royal manor here. In the 1100s King Henry I granted it and other nearby parishes to the Bishop of Lincoln. The surrounding land, except that of the Prebend, remained in Crown hands until Queen Elizabeth I sold her royal lands in the area, possibly to distance herself following her sanction of Mary Queen of Scots' execution at Fotheringhay Castle.

During the Civil War, Parliamentarian forces 'violently dispossessed the Prebendary and the vicar' and the land was sold, only to return to the Church after the Restoration in 1660. The Prebend was dissolved by an 1836 Act of Parliament, and a few years later the land passed to the Ecclesiastical Commissioners and the Prebendal Manor was sold into private hands, thus ending hundreds of years of Church ownership.

Today the manor is open to visitors by appointment only. Also to be seen is a large stone dovecote, about 24 feet square, with nests for about 700 pairs of birds. There are also gardens described by Alan Titchmarsh as a 'stunning example of a recreated medieval garden', showing the kind of high-status

The Prebendal Manor and church at Nassington.

The dovecote and part of the recreated medieval garden.

garden that might have existed between the thirteenth and fifteenth centuries. Plants include those used in medical recipes by Nicholas Colnet, physician to King Henry V at Agincourt, who occupied the manor in 1417, probably in return for his services at the battle.

5. Rockingham Castle

Rockingham Castle has been owned by the Watson family for 450 years. As the present occupier, James Saunders Watson, says, 'There are very few other homes that have been continuously occupied for nearly 1,000 years and within that time been owned by just one family since being relinquished as a royal castle.'

The castle's history begins with William the Conqueror, who in about 1070 ordered a motte and bailey to be built on this prominent hillside, with its extensive views across the Welland Valley. Later rebuilt in stone, Richard the Lionheart used the castle as a royal retreat, and his notorious brother King John often came to hunt in Rockingham Forest. The characteristic gatehouse, with its D-shaped towers, was added by King Henry III in the 1270s.

It was King Henry VIII who granted a lease on the dilapidated castle to Edward Watson in 1553, and it was transformed into a comfortable Tudor house. The freehold was bought in 1619. During the Civil War the castle became a Royalist garrison, and was captured by Cromwell's Parliamentarians; appropriately it became 'Arnescote Castle', home of the Royalist Lacey family, in the 1980s BBC drama series *By the Sword Divided*.

The Victorian owners, Richard and Lavinia Watson, were good friends with Charles Dickens, who often visited and performed in his own plays in the Long Gallery. The castle also provided some inspiration for 'Chesney Wold' in his great novel *Bleak House*, some of which was written here, as well as parts of *David Copperfield*.

Rockingham Castle and its hilltop setting, as seen from the Jurassic Way. (Julia Thorley)

Today it is still a family home, opens to the public on certain days during the summer. It is surrounded by gardens affording fine views across five counties; the remains of the medieval fortifications enclose 12 acres of lawns and gardens, with a circular rose garden on the site of the ancient keep.

The picturesque village of Rockingham, with its ancient Butter Cross, lies beneath the castle on the hillside, and gave its name to Rockingham Forest (the historic term 'forest' originally signifying an area reserved for hunting, and not necessarily covered in trees). Once covering some 200 square miles, the forest dwindled in the seventeenth century, with land sold for agriculture, and was disbanded by Act of Parliament in 1832. Today the area is administered by Rockingham Forest Trust, an environmental charity formed in 1993 and based at Stanwick Lakes, near Irthlingborough, whose aim is to 'educate, involve and inspire'.

6. Fotheringhay Castle

Rising above the meadows beside the tranquil River Nene at Fotheringhay is all that remains of a castle with a long and turbulent history. It consists of a steep-sided motte about 7 metres high and about 30 metres across, an inner bailey and the remains of the outer bailey, with surrounding ditches.

The castle is thought to have been built by Frenchman Simon de Senlis, Earl of Huntingdon and Northampton, in about 1100, as an earth and timber structure; he was married to a niece of William the Conqueror. In 1113 it passed to David, future King of Scotland, who had married Simon's widow, then was later confiscated by King John. Much later King Edward III gave it to his son Edmund Langley, Duke of York from 1385. Fotheringhay became his principal seat, and the future King Richard III was born here in 1452. In 1461 Edward of York became King Edward IV, and it became a royal castle.

It was also a state prison, and its most famous prisoner was the tragic Mary Stuart, Queen of Scots. After eighteen years of confinement around England, she spent her final days here in October 1586. She was tried, then executed in the Great Hall on 8 February 1587.

The castle was sold into private hands in 1603 and, despite its importance, by 1635 it was a ruin; popular tradition has it that Mary's son, the new King James I, ordered it to be razed to the ground. It is also claimed that the oak staircase in the Talbot Inn in nearby Oundle is that descended by the Queen to her death. Only the earthworks now remain, and upon them purple thistles grow, said to have been sown by Mary, and dubbed 'Queen Mary's Tears'. Today the site is open to the public during daylight hours.

Plaques commemorate Mary and Richard III, with fragments of castle masonry.

'Queen Mary's Tears': thistles growing on the motte at Fotheringhay.

Following the discovery of King Richard III's skeleton in Leicester in 2013, soil from the castle site was placed alongside his remains when he was reburied.

Splendid monuments to the House of York are to be found in the nearby Church of St Mary and All Saints, which was built in the 1430s by King Edward III, who also established a college there. The college and the choir of the church were demolished following the Dissolution of the Monasteries, leaving the seemingly disproportionately large church in splendid isolation.

The Church of St Mary and All Saints, Fotheringhay, and the River Nene.

7. Drayton House

In rolling Northamptonshire countryside, outside the village of Lowick near Thrapston, sits Drayton House, a family home for almost 1,000 years.

Aubrey de Vere, 1st Earl of Oxford, served the Conqueror at Hastings, and was rewarded with land to build a manor house. In the thirteenth century the family swapped 'de Vere' for 'Drayton', and the house was begun in about 1300 by Simon de Drayton. In 1328 he obtained licences to crenellate the house and enclose the park. By the late fifteenth century the house was in the hands of the Earl of Wiltshire, who entertained King Henry VII here in 1498.

Changes were made to the house in each succeeding century, and it is notable that it has never been sold, or even let. In the early sixteenth century it passed to the Barons Mordaunt, later Earls of Peterborough. The 2nd Earl's daughter, Mary, inherited it, and in 1701 she divorced her husband and married her lover. When she died his second wife was the next owner, and she left it to her cousin, who became 1st Viscount Sackville. His successor in 1770 was Charles Sackville-Germain, 5th Duke of Dorset, then in 1843 the house passed to Caroline Sackville and her husband William Bruce Stopford. Today Drayton remains in the hands of the Stopford Sackville family, who run the estate as a family business.

In 1763 the writer Horace Walpole wrote of Drayton's homely atmosphere, 'Oh, the dear old place. It is covered with portraits, crammed with old china, and not a rag in it under forty, fifty, or a thousand years old.'

The house is surrounded by well-preserved, mostly walled formal gardens, and the surrounding landscape park is crossed by avenues of trees; much new planting was done in the mid-nineteenth century, with more in recent years, including an arboretum.

This large Grade I-listed house is built around a rectangular courtyard, and the south front is visible from the drive, which doubles as a public footpath, affording fine views of the house, which sits serenely remote from any public road. It is not generally open to the public, but can be visited by special arrangement.

Also worth visiting is Lowick village (about half of which still belongs to the Drayton estate), where St Peter's church contains many tombs of the various families to have owned Drayton across the centuries.

The south forecourt at Drayton has been the principal entrance front since the seventeenth century.

St Peter's Church in Lowick contains the tombs of various owners of Drayton.

8. Deene Park

Another of the county's great houses that has been lived in continually for many centuries is Deene Park, 5 miles north-east of Corby, home of the Brudenell family for more than 500 years. The best-known Brudenell was James, 7th Earl of Cardigan, who led the infamous Charge of the Light Brigade at the Battle of Balaclava in 1854 during the Crimean War; the house contains a collection of memorabilia from Crimea, including the Earl's uniforms. (The long-sleeved woollen waistcoat, the 'cardigan', is named after him.)

The manor of Deene originally belonged to Westminster Abbey, and the annual rent of £18 was paid until 1970. Sir Robert Brudenell bought it in 1514, and it evolved thereafter to the great rambling Grade I-listed country house it is today. It is built round a spacious courtyard, which seems to have been the core of the house since earliest times. Fragments of earlier thirteenth- and fourteenth-century buildings can be seen, and a large hall was added in the fifteenth; the Great Hall of the 1570s has a fine hammerbeam roof. Further neo-Gothic building took place in the early nineteenth century, and a Ballroom was added as late as 1865.

The east front, seen in the photograph, is the most interesting; Pevsner says that it 'is completely asymmetrical, demonstrating almost every period of the architectural history of the house'.

There is a legend that King Henry VII slept here on the eve of the Battle of Bosworth.

The picturesque east front and the lake with its eighteenth-century bridge. (© Deene Park)

Outside, the formal garden, largely developed over the last thirty years, consists of a series of smaller gardens, each with its own distinctive planting. A parterre incorporates topiary 'teapots', the drink having been a passion of Edmund Brudenell, who died in 2014. Whenever he travelled abroad he took a Thermos flask and teapot with him!

The current owners are Robert and Charlotte Brudenell, Robert being the son of Edmund and Marian Brudenell, and it was they who, during their long marriage, devoted themselves to the rehabilitation of the house and park. Edmund's obituary said that 'by sheer hard work [they] brought back a near-derelict house and a bankrupt, ill-kept estate to their former glory, with the house and Marian's garden to be enjoyed by the public'.

The house, gardens and parkland are open to the public on certain days during the summer months, and the rooms viewed have a pleasant homeliness, being still used by the family and their guests.

9. Althorp Park

Another house that has been occupied by the same family for five centuries is Althorp, north-west of Northampton. Strictly, its name should be pronounced 'Awltrupp', although when the BBC Pronunciation Department contacted the present Earl the pronunciation as written – 'Althorp' – was agreed upon! It was bought from the Catesby family by John Spencer, a wealthy sheep rearer, in 1508 for £800.

Already lords of the manor of several other Northamptonshire villages, the Spencers soon developed the estate, building a red-brick Tudor house. In the early seventeenth century King Charles I visited; the house was enlarged and £1,300 spent on a banquet! Henry Spencer fought for the King at the Battle of Edgehill in 1642, but was killed by a cannonball the following year.

Now the Earls of Sunderland, Robert Spencer, the 2nd Earl, built the current house in 1688. His son Charles had a great love of books, and spent his wealth in expanding the library. His second marriage allied the family to the Churchills, Dukes of Marlborough, hence the 'Spencer' in Winston Churchill's name. The house was radically altered in the eighteenth century, when the Spencers boasted the enormous income of almost £30,000 a year, and became a centre of indulgence and festivities for the elite of the day.

By now titled the Earls Spencer, the 2nd Earl, an almost obsessive book collector, developed one of the largest private libraries in Europe, but at his death debts were escalating. The 3rd Earl lived much less extravagantly away from the estate, leaving Althorp all but abandoned, but the debts were settled.

Althorp, described by diarist John Evelyn as 'a noble uniform pile'. (© Althorp Collection)

The 5th Earl was a successful politician, but again struggled financially, and much of the library had to be sold. During the twentieth century further sales were necessary. The 7th Earl was the first to open the estate to the public, and his son the 8th Earl was a wine connoisseur (and maker) with an extensive cellar.

Althorp's current occupant, Charles, the 9th Earl, inherited a loss-making estate, but has managed to reverse its fortunes, with the house open to the public and an annual Literary Festival, founded in 2003.

The house was of course the childhood home of Diana Spencer, the future Princess of Wales, who died so tragically in August 1997. She was buried on a small island in the middle of an ornamental lake, which has inevitably become a place of pilgrimage. Thirty-six oak trees were planted along the access road, representing the years of her life, and the stable block was converted into a public exhibition devoted to her memory.

10. Fawsley Hall

In 1416 Richard Knightley, a successful Staffordshire lawyer and farmer, became Lord of the Manor of Fawsley; he evicted his peasant tenants in order to turn the parish over to sheep farming and eventually the village completely disappeared. His son, also Richard, built the earliest part of the house, the south wing. The house continued to grow, and another Richard entertained Queen Elizabeth I here in 1575.

During the Civil War, the Knightleys were sympathetic to the Parliamentarian cause, but had leased the house to Royalist sympathisers, and King Charles I was seen hunting deer here before the Battle of Naseby.

A Georgian wing was added in the eighteenth century, with Gothic alterations in the nineteenth. However, the decline in the family's fortunes thereafter was dramatic. Rainald Knightley died childless in 1895, and his widow in 1913; the house was left unoccupied and the contents auctioned in 1914.

After the Second World War the building was used by an agricultural business, then in 1966 the sixteenth-century roof was destroyed during re-roofing works. In 1975 the derelict hall was sold, and eventually opened as a hotel in 1998, so at last the public can appreciate the hall's great beauty once more.

The landscaped park, little changed since the mid-eighteenth century, has lakes and gardens, with some involvement by Capability Brown. The northern section is occupied by Badby Wood, also well worth visiting.

The hall's most famous and most unusual visitor was Joseph Merrick, the 'Elephant Man'. This tragically deformed young man was being looked after by the surgeon Frederick Treves, and Lady Knightley offered him secluded accommodation at Fawsley so that he could at least enjoy the pleasures of the countryside undisturbed. In 1887 he stayed in a cottage on the estate for six weeks; after his early years exploited as a sideshow freak, he was, according

The original sixteenth-century hall at Fawsley is flanked by larger nineteenth-century additions.

Very different architectural styles are evident in the development of Fawsley Hall.

The Brew House dates
from the sixteenth
century, built in golden
Northamptonshire sandstone.

to Treves, 'now sitting in the sun, in a clearing among the trees, arranging a bunch of violets he had gathered [during] the one supreme holiday of his life'. Leicester-born Merrick died three years later at the age of about thirty.

The main approach to the hall, as in the eighteenth century, is along a country lane off the A361.

11. Holdenby House

Another record-holder, and not only in Northamptonshire, is what was built as Holdenby Palace between 1570 and 1583 – reputedly the largest private house in Elizabethan England. The builder of Holdenby – sometimes spelled 'Holmby' and traditionally pronounced 'Homeby' – was Sir Christopher Hatton, Lord Chancellor and devoted favourite of Queen Elizabeth I. The Hattons had been here since the fifteenth century, and their manor house was demolished to make way for the new building.

This prodigious Palace, with 123 mullioned windows and two courtyards, was constructed specifically to honour Hatton's beloved Queen in expectation of a royal visit; it was reputed to have covered approximately 7,300 square metres. When he died in 1591 he was childless and bankrupt, having bought Kirby Hall (*see* entry 12) while Holdenby was still being built.

The house was bought by King James I, who used it as a favourite summer residence. However, for his son, King Charles I, it became a prison following the Civil War; he lived here in almost royal state for several months in 1647.

After the war the Palace was sold to the Parliamentarian Captain Adam Baynes, who demolished most of it except for a single small domestic wing, and sold the materials. It then briefly became royal property again after the

Today's Holdenby, once reputedly the largest private house in Elizabethan England. (Courtesy of Holdenby House)

Restoration in 1660, then in 1709 was bought by the Duke of Marlborough, who sold it to the Clifden family, since when it has descended down the female line to the present owners, the Lowthers.

The Grade II*-listed building as it exists today was built in a style reminiscent of the original by the present owners' great-great-grandmother, Lady Clifden, in the 1870s, incorporating some of the remains of the old mansion. Although enlarged again in the 1880s, it is still no more than about one-eighth of the extent of the original Palace. All that remains of Hatton's work are two isolated late sixteenth-century archways that once led to the courtyards.

The house is surrounded by a 20-acre Grade I-listed garden, including formal gardens and a rare original Elizabethan terraced rose garden.

In July 2011 the exterior of Holdenby House was transformed as the location of Miss Havisham's 'Satis House' in the BBC adaptation of Dickens's *Great Expectations*. House and gardens are open to the public on certain days between April and September.

12. Kirby Hall

In 1575, while Holdenby Palace was still being built, Christopher Hatton purchased Kirby Hall from Sir Humphrey Stafford of Blatherwick, who had begun it in 1570. Earlier the estate had been partly owned by the Augustinian priors of Fineshade and the Brudenell family of Deene Park. Stafford's son, also Humphrey, became Sheriff of Northamptonshire in 1566 and needed a house to suit his new status. The new house was still unfinished when sold to Hatton.

Hatton had properties elsewhere and, despite his wealth, he left Kirby Hall to languish; it was some eight years before he even visited it. When he died in 1591 a distant relation, another Sir Christopher, inherited the house, and entertained King James I on several occasions. He engaged Inigo Jones to modernise the outmoded Elizabethan house in a novel, modern, symmetrical style. Basically a two-storeyed, richly decorated courtyard house, Nikolaus Pevsner considered it one of the most important and interesting English houses of its time.

However, the Hattons fell on hard times, and Kirby Hall was sold to the Crown in 1608. By the middle of the eighteenth century it had become neglected, and when the Hattons departed in 1764 it passed to the Finch-Hatton family. Despite some refurbishment after 1786, by the early nineteenth century the gardens had been abandoned and the house was soon in a ruinous state.

In 1930 the remains came under the care of the Ministry of Works, and some restoration began. The Finch-Hattons' descendants, the Earls of Winchilsea, still retain the estate today, and the Grade I-listed house is managed by English Heritage. Much is roofless, but the walls of many of the great rooms remain intact and the gardens have been recently restored. The Great Garden of the early seventeenth century was recreated in the 1990s following excavation and documentary research. It has a lawn 120 metres long with gravel paths in a late seventeenth-century style adapted from a design at Longleat.

Kirby Hall appeared in the 1999 adaptation of Jane Austen's *Mansfield Park* as well as Steve Coogan's *Tristram Shandy: A Cock and Bull Story* in 2005. The BBC's *Antiques Roadshow* visited in 2014.

The nearer portion of Kirby Hall is the only part still roofed and glazed. (With thanks to English Heritage)

13. Sulgrave Manor

This house is associated with another prominent statesman, but in this case not an English one. It was built by Lawrence Washington, George Washington's five times great-grandfather, in 1539, and parts of the original Tudor house can still be seen.

At the Dissolution of the Monasteries in 1538, St Andrew's Priory was acquired by the Crown, then sold to Lawrence Washington, a wool merchant and former Mayor of Northampton. The family retained the manor until 1659, when it was sold. Meanwhile one of Lawrence's descendents, John Washington of Essex, emigrated to Virginia, and his great-grandson was George Washington (1732–1799), first President of the United States in 1789. Sulgrave still bears the family's coat of arms depicting the stars and stripes that are thought to have influenced the American flag.

In around 1673 the house was rebuilt and enlarged, and in about 1780 the west part of the original house was demolished. By the mid-nineteenth century Sulgrave Manor had become a dilapidated farmhouse, until bought by public subscription in 1914. The initiative came from the British American Peace Committee set up in 1911 in the USA to commemorate a century of peace between Britain and the USA since the Treaty of Ghent of 1814.

English architect and landscape designer Sir Reginald Blomfield restored the house and garden between 1920 and 1930, and it was then also opened to the public. The garden, of which nothing remained, was remade and is still largely

Sulgrave Manor, a symbol of the close historical connection between Britain and America. (Sulgrave Manor)

A bust of George Washington in the garden at Sulgrave. (Sulgrave Manor)

unaltered today, containing topiary, an orchard and a herb garden. In 1921 the Sulgrave Manor Trust was established to care for the house and promote goodwill between the two countries.

Since 1997 the Grade I-listed building has been administered by the Sulgrave Manor Board and is used for educational programmes describing the manor's history and agricultural environment, including regular re-enactments.

Sadly, in recent times the buildings have been found to be in further need of repair and conservation, and in 2014 the bicentenary of the Treaty of Ghent was used to launch a fundraising appeal, resulting in grants from the States to allow rethatching. The manor is also supported by the Friends of Sulgrave Manor, a group of American women.

On the manor's website Dr Steven Knapp, President of George Washington University, Washington DC, is quoted as saying: 'There is no richer symbol of the deep historical and cultural connection between our two nations than the ancestral home of the leading founder of the United States.'

14. Castle Ashby

While Christopher Hatton was building his great Palace at Holdenby, Henry Compton was beginning work on Castle Ashby House. In 1512 the manor had been bought by Sir William Compton of Compton Wynyates in Warwickshire, a close friend of King Henry VIII. Later, in 1574, the medieval castle was pulled down and the new house begun. It was E-shaped, to celebrate the coronation of Queen Elizabeth I.

William's son, also William, was created Earl of Northampton in 1618; in 1584 he had married Elizabeth Spencer, whose inherited fortune financed further rebuilding and extravagant entertaining, with many royal visits; at that time the household had eighty-three servants and four chaplains!

Alterations followed in the sixteenth and seventeenth centuries, and when the front was rebuilt in a neo-Jacobean style, an unusual lettered balustrade was added around the parapet. Attributed to Inigo Jones, it reads in Latin: 'Except the Lord build the house they labour but in vain that build it; except the Lord keep the house the watchman waketh but in vain.'

When Charles, the 7th Earl, undertook the Grand Tour he met Robert Adam in Italy. Both Adam and Capability Brown were invited to produce designs for improving the park; between 1761 and 1774 the grounds were altered to produce a less formal outlook, although the remaining 'Grande Avenue' to the south still stretches for 3½ miles.

The 8th Earl also spent lavishly, but when the 9th Earl (who became the 1st Marquess of Northampton in 1812) inherited the property it was in need of urgent repairs. He, and later his son, spent long periods abroad, especially in Italy.

The present glorious gardens were developed from 1862 by the 3rd Marquess; the main gardens are known collectively as The Terraces, and contain much terracotta work from a factory in Stamford, again incorporating biblical inscriptions. At about the same time the park was almost doubled in size to about 1,000 acres.

Castle Ashby, with its unusual Latin inscription running round the balustrade.

The magnificent Orangery incorporates work by the Victorian architects Matthew Digby Wyatt and William Burges.

Castle Ashby House has recently been passed to Earl Compton, the son of the 7th Marquess, while the Marquess himself continues the family tradition of managing the Castle Ashby and Compton Wynyates estates.

15. Rushton Hall

The Tresham family has already been encountered at Newton-in-the-Willows. William Tresham, a loyal servant of King Henry V who fought with him at Agincourt, bought the Rushton estate in 1438 and began to build his new family home. Knighted for his services, he was a local MP and Sheriff of the county. Sir William's son Thomas took over the project on his father's death, and the resulting hall is a magnificent and richly decorated building.

Although serving the Protestant Kings Henry VIII and Edward VI, Thomas remained a Catholic and supported the new Queen Mary Tudor, for which he was richly rewarded.

Thomas's grandson, also Thomas, inherited Rushton in 1559 when he was just nine years old. When later knighted at Kenilworth by Queen Elizabeth I and asked to denounce Catholicism, he refused and was imprisoned for twelve years, during which time he conceived the Triangular Lodge (*see* entry 16). A keen builder, he enlarged the hall considerably, including a priest hole and a secret escape tunnel for priests.

Thomas's son Francis was also a fervent Catholic, twice convicted for treason, and with his cousin Robert Catesby was involved in planning and financing the Gunpowder Plot of 1605 (*see* entry 34). When the plot was discovered, Francis was sentenced to death, but died in the Tower of London in December 1605.

His son Lewis was just as reckless, and mounting debts led to Rushton Hall being handed to the Crown. It was then sold to Sir William Cockayne, Lord Mayor of London, who expanded it further. In 1731 the estate was sold to the Hopes, a Dutch banking family.

In 1853 Miss Clara Thornhill bought Rushton. Charles Dickens was a great friend and visited many times. It is thought that he conceived the idea of the interior of Miss Havisham's 'Satis House' in *Great Expectations* during one of his visits.

When Clara's husband, William Clarke-Thornhill, died in 1934, the hall was let to various tenants, then was bought by G. H. Pain. It was he who transferred the Triangular Lodge to the care of the Ministry of Works, now English Heritage.

In 1959 the Royal National Institute for the Blind bought the house for £1, and it became a school for the blind. When the RNIB moved out in 2003, the new owners transformed the magnificent Grade I-listed hall into a four Red Star hotel boasting the county's only three-rosette restaurant and luxury spa.

The seventeenth-century east front of Rushton Hall.

The south side of the house dates from 1848.

16. The Triangular Lodge

Standing in what was once the garden of Rushton Hall is one of Northamptonshire's – indeed, England's – most unusual buildings. It was built by Sir Thomas Tresham between 1593 and 1597, and reflects and symbolises his strong Catholic faith. He had just been released after twelve years in prison for refusing to embrace Protestantism, and the lodge was intended as a reaffirmation of his beliefs.

The basis of the building is the number three, signifying the Holy Trinity. It has three floors and three sides, each with three gables surmounted by triangular obelisks and decorated with religious emblems, and groups of three windows. The basement windows are small trefoils in shape (the trefoil – three leaves, clover-like – was the Tresham emblem). The ground-floor windows are lozenge-shaped with twelve small circular openings, while the windows on the first floor are the largest, again trefoil in shape. The walls are surmounted by three gargoyles, and there is also a triangular chimney.

The entrance, approached by steps, is on the south-east side, and bears the inscription '*Tres Testimonium Dant*' ('There are three that give witness'), a quotation from St John's Gospel – but it also incorporates a nice pun, as Tresham's wife called him by the pet name 'Tres' in her letters. One wall bears

Rushton Triangular Lodge: 'no more nor less than a profession of faith'. (With thanks to English Heritage)

the number '15', another '93', and the third 'TT'. In addition, each side bears a Biblical quotation, each thirty-three letters long.

The main room on each floor is hexagonal, leaving a triangular space in each corner; two are small rooms, while the third contains a spiral staircase.

The Grade I-listed Triangular Lodge was the only building Tresham designed that was completed in his lifetime (*see* also entry 17). 'A folly? A bauble? A pretty conceit?' asks Pevsner. No; it is 'no more nor less than a profession of faith', to be looked at 'with respect', and this can still be done as the lodge is now cared for by English Heritage and open to the public.

17. Lyveden

With its unglazed, roofless shell silhouetted against the sky, Lyveden (sometimes known as 'Lyveden New Bield' – 'New Build') has all the appearance of a ruin, but in fact it is an unfinished building, another of the faith-inspired designs of Catholic Sir Thomas Tresham.

The family already owned Lyveden Manor House (the 'Old Bield'), acquired in about 1540. Above the manor on a level grassy plateau commanding panoramic views Tresham planned a building full of religious symbolism based around the numbers three, five, seven and nine; for example, the windows are 5 feet high, with five faces and bays at 5 feet from each corner of the building, the number five commonly representing Jesus. The number three, the Trinity, is again also significant. Around the exterior are friezes decorated with religious symbols, some still undeciphered.

Despite its size, Lyveden was probably not intended for full-time occupation, but as a 'garden lodge' or 'banqueting house', popular at the time as somewhere the owner could live simply with minimal staff for a time while his main house was being thoroughly cleaned.

Tresham designed extensive gardens between his manor house and the New Bield, through which visitors could walk on a kind of 'metaphorical pilgrimage'. The gardens have recently been recreated by the National Trust, and include a moat, labyrinth, orchard and 'snail mounts', viewing hillocks climbed by spiral paths.

The shell of Lyveden New Bield, seen from across the moat in the gardens.

Work began in 1595, and two years later part of the ground floor was complete. The following year Tresham was again imprisoned for four years, but continued to issue instructions for his new building. He also paid fines totalling £8,000 between 1581 and 1605.

When he died in September 1605 all work ceased. Three months later his older son, the Gunpowder Plotter Francis, died in the Tower of London. His younger son Lewis inherited, but, as one writer puts it, his 'rapid rise in social rank was matched only by his speedy descent into debt.' By the end of the Civil War the estate had been lost, and changed hands several times until acquired by the National Trust in 1922. It is now Grade I listed and open to the public.

One writer likens Lyveden to 'a doll's house awaiting furniture and a family to move into it'. But that will never happen, and the incomplete building stands more or less as it was left by the builders 400 years ago, a monument to one man's unswervable faith.

18. Apethorpe Palace

Begun in the late fifteenth century and originally styled Apethorpe Hall – pronounced 'Apthorp' – the main house was built around three courtyards and is considered one of the finest Jacobean mansions in England, incorporating elements from almost every period of English architecture. One architectural historian describes it as 'almost like a small town of its own'.

King Henry VIII acquired the house in the early sixteenth century. Queen Elizabeth I inherited it, and Sir Walter Mildmay, her Chancellor of the Exchequer, bought it in 1551. In 1622 it was extended with new staterooms, the last complete and original set left in England. It also features some of the most important surviving plasterwork and fireplaces of the period. It then passed to another branch of the family, the Fanes, later Earls of Westmorland, for a further 300 years.

The Westmorlands' financial difficulties forced a sale in 1904. After the Second World War the house was sold to manufacturer Leonard Brassey and given a sensitive upgrading by the architect Reginald Blomfield (*see* entry 13). In the late 1940s it became a Catholic approved school, and several ugly additions were made. A controversial purchase in 1983 left the house empty, neglected and decaying, and it became dangerously unsafe. Its loss to the nation's heritage would have been catastrophic, and in 1998 it was one of the first buildings on English Heritage's Buildings at Risk Register, resulting in a rare compulsory purchase by the Government in 2004. Handed over to English Heritage, £8 million was spent to make the forty-eight-bedroom house waterproof, and it was offered for sale, albeit with no plumbing, power or heating. At the end of 2014 French anglophile Baron von Pfetten bought it, committing his family to its restoration and refurbishment and to fifty days' public opening a year for eighty years. He also agreed to rename the house Apethorpe Palace, due to its royal ownership, a title that many believe it doesn't merit. Nonetheless, visitors can now enjoy pre-booked tours of this magnificent Grade I-listed building in July and August.

The Baron and his wife Nadia, a conservation architect, spent many years renovating their château in France, and will use this experience at Apethorpe. 'Our vision for Apethorpe is to help this house regain the place in British history that it deserves.' Nadia adds, 'The first time that I saw this house, I fell in love with it. You can feel the generations that have gone before.'

19. Lamport Hall

Lamport Hall was the home of the Isham family for more than 400 years. In 1568 wool merchant John Isham built the original manor house, then his grandson, also John, became the first baronet in 1627. In 1655 Sir Justinian Isham built the main existing building, designed by John Webb, a pupil of Inigo Jones, in the then new Italian style. The south-west and north fronts were added in 1741, and the south-east front in 1842.

Sir Charles Isham inherited the house in 1846. He was a keen gardener and in 1847 created one of the first rockeries in England, which still exists today; 90 feet long, it rises up 24 feet like a ruined castle. It was populated by the world's first terracotta garden gnomes, imported from Germany. Legend has it that after Sir Charles's death the gnomes became targets for his daughters' air rifles, but happily one of the originals survived and is on view in the hall.

The house also contains an outstanding collection of paintings and furniture, and an eighteenth-century library; one of its treasures is King Charles I's 1638 Bible. Many of the contents were collected during the 3rd Baronet's Grand Tour of Europe in the 1670s.

From the second half of the nineteenth century the former family home was successively divided into flats, used as a hunting box, a country club, home of the county Record Office, an army base and an Italian prisoner of war camp. Consequently by the 1950s Lamport Hall was in poor condition, so its owner, Sir Gyles Isham, the 12th Baronet, undertook major renovation works. In 1974 he allowed the ground floor to be opened to the public.

On his death, having no heir, he left the house and its contents to the Lamport Hall Preservation Trust, which he had set up. This is a charitable organisation,

Above: The Isham motto 'In things transitory resteth no glory' appears over the entrance portico.

Below: The south-west wing at Lamport, dating from 1741.

established to ensure Lamport's survival for the enjoyment of visitors and as a centre of culture and education. It also offers Royal Horticultural Society gardening courses. This new role for the house is very appropriate, as the Isham family had a long tradition of interest in education, for both sexes.

Another feature of Lamport is the small yet fascinating Museum of Rural Life, a working museum operated by the Hannington Vintage Tractor Club.

20. Boughton House

Boughton House, dubbed 'the English Versailles', is one of the seats of the Montagu-Douglas-Scott family, Dukes of Buccleuch. Although medieval in origin, today's house has very much the air of a French château, unlike any other English country house. Its opulence arises from the union of three great families: the Dukes of Montagu, the Dukes of Queensberry (the Douglases) and the Dukes of Buccleuch (the Scotts).

Sir Edward Montagu bought and converted the original monastic building in 1528. In 1647 King Charles I visited to play bowls while under arrest at Holdenby (*see* entry 11). Ralph Montagu, the 1st Duke, an ambitious politician as well as a passionate patron of the arts, inherited the simple Tudor house in 1683, and most of the present French-influenced building is his work, using Huguenot craftspeople (he was several times Ambassador to France). Days, weeks and months inform the plan: it is built around seven courtyards, with twelve entrances, fifty-two chimney stacks and 365 windows.

The 2nd Duke's daughter Mary married George Brudenell of Deene (*see* entry 8), the 4th Earl of Cardigan, in whose favour the duchy of Montagu was recreated in 1766. Then in 1790 Boughton passed by marriage to the Scottish Dukes of Buccleuch, but after 1749 was little used, so remains almost unaltered from that time; it still has some of the best preserved state rooms of the period. In the early twentieth century the 8th Duke and Duchess made the house a family home once again. Visiting in 1945, the American-born British politician and diarist Sir Henry 'Chips' Channon described Boughton as 'a dream house with a strange, sleepy quality, but its richness, its beauty and possessions are stupefying ... But it is the stillness, the curious quiet of Boughton that impresses the most.'

In the 1980s the 9th Duke began the process of opening the house to the public. On show is one of Britain's most outstanding collections of fine art, furniture, tapestries, porcelain and carpets, as well as paintings by the great masters, and an armoury.

The house is surrounded by formal eighteenth-century landscaped gardens, created by the 1st Duke. The 2nd Duke, nicknamed 'John the Planter', continued to develop and adapt them to his own tastes with water features, splendid vistas and tree-lined avenues. During the time that the house 'slept' the gardens became neglected, but happily their restoration continues today under the present Duke. Boughton has featured as a film location, including *Les Miserables* in 2013.

Boughton House: 'the English Versailles'.

Boughton from the air. (Sarah Vivienne, courtesy of Boughton House)

21. Canons Ashby

It is hard to believe that at the end of the 1970s Canons Ashby House was close to collapse and the gardens had become a meadow. Happily, in 1981 the property passed to the National Trust, which has cared for it ever since.

The original manor used stone from the Augustinian priory of about 1150, from which it gets its name, and which was a victim of the Dissolution of the Monasteries in 1536. Eventually it passed by marriage to the Drydens of Cumbria, and from 1550 John Dryden built a completely new house, incorporating part of a medieval farmhouse, a modest two-storey building around a small cobbled courtyard; the central tower dates from about 1550. The house was completed in the 1590s by John's son Erasmus, and is noted for its Tudor wall paintings and Jacobean plasterwork. It was further altered considerably by Edward Dryden in the eighteenth century. (Edward was a nephew of the poet John Dryden, also a Northamptonshire native born in the rectory at Aldwincle in east Northamptonshire in 1631.)

Edward laid out the terraced gardens in 1708–10, and they had a strong influence on the early twentieth-century Arts & Crafts garden movement popularised by Gertrude Jekyll and architect Edward Lutyens.

Canons Ashby has remained essentially unchanged since 1710, and is now seen as it was when occupied by the Victorian antiquary and amateur architect Sir Henry Dryden, who owned the house for sixty-one years and whose records have helped with the restoration of the gardens.

In 1981 Gervase Jackson-Stops, Architectural Adviser to the National Trust, fought for the rescue of the then decaying manor house – it was the first time that the Trust used government funds rather than the traditional family endowment to save a historic house.

The house is surrounded by colourful formal gardens, and boasts an orchard containing sixteenth-century fruit tree varieties. Nearby is the Priory Church, the only remaining feature of the monastery; it represents just the west end of the nave of the abbey church, giving some idea of the enormous size of the original; it is today one of only four private churches in England, and contains many memorials to Dryden family members. It was the scene of a Civil War skirmish when the Roundheads took to the tower to fight off a party of Royalists.

Canons Ashby and, beyond, the Priory Church, the only remaining feature of the monastery.

Historic Churches

22. St Michael & All Angels, Wadenhoe

The small and picturesque village of Wadenhoe, north of Thrapston beside the River Nene, stands on the Nene Way long-distance footpath (*see* entry 50).

The parish church, part of the Oundle Deanery, stands on a hill above the river and village, and unusually is also dedicated St Giles, making it one of only a few in the country with a double dedication; there is a banner to St Giles in the chancel.

The distinctive late Norman saddle-back tower, one of only a few left in the county, is all that survives of a twelfth-century church, the chancel and nave having been rebuilt sometime in the thirteenth century. It is built in three stages with diagonal angle buttresses and a roof is tiled with Collyweston stone. The tower contains a peal of six bells.

Despite extensive restoration in 1901, the interior contains architectural detail from the thirteenth and fourteenth centuries, including windows and the arch to the nave. The font also dates from the thirteenth century. The oak pulpit is early eighteenth century, and the seating is mostly modern, although some carved pew ends in the aisles are possibly from the sixteenth century.

A brass plate commemorates Miss Brittle, who was headmistress of the former Church of England village school for nearly fifty years. There are also memorials to members of the Hunt family, long associated with Wadenhoe. One records the deaths of Thomas and Caroline Welch Hunt, who were murdered by bandits while honeymooning in Italy in 1824. One of the windows is in memory of the Right Honourable George Ward-Hunt, who was MP for Northamptonshire for twenty years and Chancellor of the Exchequer in Disraeli's cabinet in 1868. Some of the gold braid from his Chancellor's robes was incorporated in the present altar cloth. It is said that Wadenhoe was the first village in England to have a telegraph Post Office (only closed in relatively recent years) at the request of Ward-Hunt so he could be kept abreast of the latest news.

Being on a hillside the churchyard falls away to the east and contains tombs and headstones dating back to the seventeenth century.

The church appears on film during the opening scenes of the 1999 TV movie adaptation of *A Christmas Carol* starring Patrick Stewart.

Wadenhoe church has a rare late Norman saddle-back tower.

St Michael & All Angels, Wadenhoe, on its hilltop site.

23. All Saints, Brixworth

The village of Brixworth, north of Northampton, is well known for one of the most important Romanesque churches in Europe, and England's largest surviving Anglo-Saxon building.

The church has been in continuous use for Christian worship for some 1,300 years, since the foundation of a monastery by the monks of Peterborough in the seventh century; the present church dates from about AD 750–850. After damage by invading Vikings, it was restored in the tenth century, at which time the clerestory windows we see today were added.

The nave is entirely from the Saxon period, and at the base of what is now the tower a doorway would have led into the 'narthex', an entrance porch where much of the church business and ceremonies would have taken place. The distinctive turret containing the tower stairs was added in the eleventh century, and is one of only four like it surviving in England.

Inside the church is simple and uncluttered. Originally the nave and chancel were separated by a wall with arches and doorways; Brixworth may have been the first church to 'screen' the chancel from the nave in this way. The present chancel arch is fourteenth century, but the remnants of the side arches can still be seen.

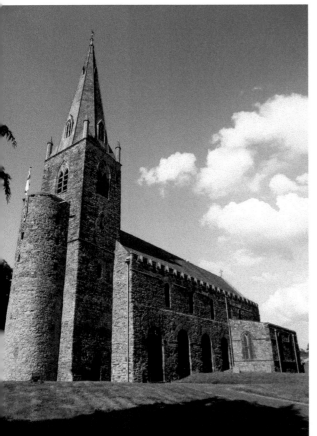

Brixworth church's distinctive turret on the tower was added in the eleventh century.

There is a ring crypt around the apse at the east end of the church, one of only three of its kind in Europe; it is thought to have provided an ambulatory, or walkway, for pilgrims to view a relic set in the wall.

The so-called 'Brixworth Relic' was discovered in 1809 when workmen were making alterations to the thirteenth-century Lady Chapel. Inside a fourteenth-century stone relic container was a wooden box containing a small human throat bone wrapped in cloth; the cloth may have borne the name of the saint to whom the bone belonged, but it disintegrated on exposure to the air, so the bone's owner remains a mystery. One theory is that it might have belonged to St Boniface, who was popular in the village in medieval times.

This historically important church is open for visitors during the hours of daylight, and guided tours can be arranged.

Since 1983 the church has been cared for by the Friends of All Saints, who acquired the Thomas Roe Charity School building in Church Street and, after much work, opened it as a Heritage Centre in 1995, containing displays relating to both the church and the village.

24. All Saints, Earls Barton

Another exceptional church dedicated to All Saints, and another with noteworthy Saxon origins, is that of the large shoemaking village of Earls Barton, east of Northampton (the Earls in question were the Earls of Huntingdon).

It is the tenth-century tower that singles out this building, its superb stonework and carving making it one of the best examples of Saxon architecture in England. The tower, with its Roman-influenced design, constructed of stone rubble and rendered, dates from around 970, and is all that remains of a church that was just a tower, with the nave in the base and a small eastern extension serving as a chancel. The upper floors were possibly accommodation for the priest (perhaps also a place of refuge from invaders), with a belfry in the uppermost storey.

In the late twelfth century the present nave and chancel were added, forming the building we see today. This may have been done by Simon de Senlis, Earl of Northampton, who we have already encountered at Fotheringhay.

Despite its age, the foundations of the tower are only 8–12 inches thick, and it rises to well over 60 feet, each storey successively thinner. It probably originally had a pyramidal roof. At the corners are distinctive long vertical and short horizontal quoins, and many pilasters and strapwork in limestone adorn the walls; it almost looks like medieval timber-framing in stone.

The west doorway at the foot of the tower is built from thick slabs placed on end, extending through the thickness of the wall. On each side of the tower are

Earls Barton's tower is one of the best examples of Saxon architecture in England.
*Inset:*A close-up of the tower, with its distinctive limestone pilasters and strapwork.

numerous belfry openings, a very rare feature and suggesting that All Saints may always have had bells in the tower.

Inside the church are many thirteenth-century features, while the chancel arch is Early English, and the painted screen dates from the fifteenth century, decorated with saints and butterflies, the latter being symbolic of resurrection. The painting was done in 1935 by artist Henry Bird, also responsible for the Safety Curtain in Northampton's Royal Theatre (*see* entry 30). The west end of the chancel is Norman, with a thirteenth-century priest's door, and the windows range from Early English to Perpendicular Gothic.

All in all, this is one of the most remarkable Saxon churches to survive in England, and is normally open during daylight hours.

25. Holy Trinity, Rothwell

Known locally as 'Rowell', in 1204 King John granted permission for a weekly market and annual fair at Rothwell, and both continue to this day. Thomas Tresham was responsible for the town's Market Hall, the third of his trilogy of faith-inspired buildings, being cross-shaped (see Rushton Hall and the Triangular Lodge). It stood unfinished for 300 years.

Dating from the twelfth century, Holy Trinity church was owned by the wealthy Augustinian abbey at Cirencester, and was once much larger than it is today. Following the Dissolution of the Monasteries the church's fortunes declined; it fell into disrepair and the spire was struck by lightning in 1660, crashing down into the building. The north and south transepts were subsequently demolished, then in 1750 an earthquake caused further damage. By the early nineteenth century it was reported that the church was no longer fit for worship, its sole purpose being to house the town's fire engine! Extensive restoration took place during the twentieth century.

At 173 feet, Holy Trinity is the longest parish church in Northamptonshire, but its main claim to fame is said to have been accidentally discovered in about 1700 by a gravedigger who fell through a buried window into a previously unknown thirteenth-century charnel house, or ossuary, beneath the south aisle, which contained the remains of about 2,500 individuals.

The crypt has since been reorganised, with most of the skulls displayed on shelves around the walls, and others, together with predominantly femurs, in two wooden enclosures in the centre. Theories about the origins of the remains include Danes slain by Saxons in battle, victims of the nearby Battle of Naseby, a monastic burial, or victims of a plague epidemic, but these have since been discounted. Another theory, also debunked, was that the preponderance of femurs and skulls reflected the belief that these were the only bones required by the church for resurrection.

A more recent suggestion is that the crypt, which once had windows, was a medieval monument for pilgrims and villagers who prayed among the bones of their ancestors. Once there may have been hundreds of such bone crypts, but the only other surviving one is at Hythe in Kent. The Rothwell remains were possibly moved into the crypt from graves, including some from different cemeteries.

The crypt is open to the public on Sunday afternoons in the summer, but it is worth checking beforehand if you intend to visit.

Similar in appearance to Lyveden is Tresham's Market Hall, another of his faith-inspired buildings.

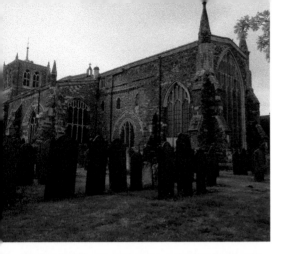

Holy Trinity, Rothwell, is the longest parish church in Northamptonshire.

Predominantly skulls and femurs fill the unusual and mysterious ossuary below Holy Trinity.

26. St Mary's, Higham Ferrers

Higham Ferrers is a historic town with many fine old buildings lining the A6 London–Carlisle road. There was a castle here in the eleventh century, and the town later became the property of John of Gaunt, Duke of Lancaster. It remains part of the Duchy of Lancaster today.

The church, one of the finest in the county, dates from the thirteenth century. In the fifteenth century further building took place under the auspices of Bishop Henry Chichele. Born in Higham in 1363, he was mayor several times, then entered the Church and in 1413 became Archbishop of Canterbury for thirty years.

In about 1630 the spire and part of the tower collapsed. Following rebuilding, it has since been described as 'one of the finest in a county famous for spires'.

The remarkable deeply recessed west porch is thought to have been the work of French masons employed in the rebuilding of Westminster Abbey. The doors are surmounted by the Virgin Mary, flanked by scrolls, leaves and flowers, and scenes from the life of Christ. Inside, the church has an unusually spacious double nave and aisles, many fine memorials, and twenty 'miserere' seats in the chancel given by Archbishop Chichele.

In the twentieth century generous benefactors continued to embellish the building. For example, the fine roof bosses were redecorated in memory of

Below left: St Mary's, Higham Ferrers: 'one of the finest in a county famous for spires'.

Below right: In the west porch the Virgin Mary is flanked by scenes from the life of Christ.

The Chantry Chapel was used as a grammar school between 1542 and 1906.

The remains of Chichele College, founded in 1431.

John White, a local prominent shoe manufacturer, and the inner west porch glass doors are in memory of his wife.

Beside the west door is the Chantry Chapel, Grade I listed like the church. Re-established in 1422 by Archbishop Chichele, it was used as a grammar school between 1542 and 1906 and was rededicated as a chantry chapel in 1942. At the west end there is a statue of Chichele.

Across the churchyard is the Grade I-listed Bede House, or almshouse, again founded by Chichele in about 1428 and restored in the nineteenth century. This distinctive building has alternating courses of limestone and ironstone, and retains its original timber roof frame and large open fireplace. It originally accommodated twelve poor men of the parish, and a woman to care for them; it is now used as the church hall.

A little further north along the main street are the remains of a college founded by Chichele in 1431. It was lost at the Dissolution of the Monasteries, but the remains survive under the care of English Heritage.

Northampton

27. St Peter's Church

The town of Northampton is steeped in history. It was an important place in the Middle Ages, with a royal castle and palace. The trial of Archbishop Thomas à Becket took place in the castle, as well as many councils and parliaments, and the first scene of Shakespeare's *King John* is set there.

Standing between the site of the Anglo-Saxon palace of about AD 800 and the scant remains of the Norman castle (a re-erected stone gateway near the Castle railway station that now occupies the site) is the Grade I-listed St Peter's Church, considered the most outstanding and interesting Norman church in the county. It was probably built in the twelfth century by Simon de Senlis II. In 1607 the west tower fell but was rebuilt later in a slightly different position. In the 1850s the church was restored by the great Gothic architect George Gilbert Scott; he rebuilt the east end and lowered the nave floor by a foot in order to provide steps up to the chancel; prior to that there was, unusually, no division between the nave and the chancel, suggesting that the church may have had a special connection with the castle next door.

St Peter's is considered the most outstanding Norman church in the county.

Above the Norman arcades are corbels carved with human and animal heads, each unique.

St Peter's is built of reddish ironstone and yellowish limestone, often alternated for decorative effect. Along the north and south sides are Norman arcades, above which are twelfth-century corbels carved with a variety of human and animal heads, each unique. Among the memorials inside is one to William Smith, the 'Father of English Geology', who died in 1839 and is buried in the churchyard.

Sadly the church closed in 1995 and since 1998 has been in the care of the Churches Conservation Trust. The interior was suffering from mould, cured by low-level heating, while the removal of layers of paint and Victorian additions revealed the original decoration. Today the building is used as a community asset, and although it is not open regularly a key can be obtained locally. On display inside are some remnants of the church, including an early carved grave slab that may be linked to St Ragener, who is associated with the church. During the reign of Edward the Confessor a shrine was built to him, and the church thus became a place of pilgrimage, and many miracles are said to have taken place.

28. All Saints' Church

Simon de Senlis was also responsible for All Hallows' Church, as it was then known. But disaster struck Northampton on 20 September 1675, when most of the old town was destroyed by fire, including the church.

After the fire, according to the inscription around the front of the new church, King Charles II 'gave a thousand tun of timber towards the rebuilding of this church and to this town seven years chimney money collected in it.' This was achieved by the Earl of Northampton, a friend of the King, despite Northampton having supported Parliament during the not-so-distant Civil War! The timber came from the Royal forests of Salcey and Rockingham. One-tenth of the money collected to rebuild the town went to the new church, which was similar to Sir Christopher Wren's designs following the Fire of London a decade earlier.

Above: All Saints' Church: 'one of the stateliest of its date outside London', says Pevsner.

Right: On the portico is a statue of King Charles II, in Roman tunic and flowing wig.

Built on the remains of the old church (the tower and crypt), which was twice the length of its successor, the new building was almost square in plan with a dome at the centre lit by a lantern above. The Mayoral Seat dominates the pews on the south side, and in the north aisle there is a Consistory Court, previously located in the space now occupied by the coffee shop.

All Saints is one of the few English parish churches to have a Consistory, or Ecclesiastical, Court (all dioceses have them). These were established by William the Conqueror, but today have lost much of their traditional role; they mainly deal with churchyards and church property, but can also try certain clergy accused of misconduct.

The new building was consecrated and opened in 1680. The large portico was added in 1701, as a memorial to the King's contribution, and carries a statue of him. At noon on Oak Apple Day (commemorating the King's concealment in an oak tree following his defeat at the Battle of Worcester in 1651) the choir sings from the roof as the statue is wreathed in oak leaves.

Pevsner says that the new church was highly admired at the time, 'and is indeed one of the stateliest of its date outside London.'

In 2008 the west front was refurbished, with a coffee shop; the north end is named the John Clare Lounge, after the poet who once sat outside, composing his poems, having wandered down from the asylum where he lived.

29. The Guildhall

By the middle of the nineteenth century Northampton's old town hall (between Abington Street and Wood Hill) had become too small, so a competition was held for a new building in St Giles Square. The winner was architect Edward Godwin, who was only twenty-eight at the time, and the Guildhall was built between 1861 and 1864 in a wonderful neo-Gothic style.

The Grade II*-listed building accommodates Borough Council offices and is also used for weddings and civil partnerships. It also used to include a courtroom, and there are still prison cells in the large basement. A hidden room in the attic, possibly once the home of a caretaker, is accessed by a secret staircase.

At the centre of the Guildhall is the impressive Great Hall, its walls decorated in 1925 with portraits of famous men associated with the town. There are also murals painted by Henry Bird in 1949 entitled 'The Muses Contemplating Northampton'. (Bird was also responsible for the Safety Curtain in the Royal Theatre – *see* entry 30.)

The Guildhall was extended westwards in 1889–92 in the same style, so that the join is barely noticeable. One hundred years later, in 1992, a modern

Northampton's Gothic
Guildhall, built in 1861–64.

The Great Hall, its walls
carrying portraits of famous
men associated with the town.

extension was made eastwards, built around a courtyard. This building is in a
strikingly modern style, but is cleverly very much in keeping with the original;
the design choice was decided by public ballot. In the lobby is a statue of Spencer
Perceval, MP for Northampton in 1796 and the only British Prime Minister to
have been assassinated, shot in the lobby of the Houses of Parliament in 1812
by a bankrupt Liverpool broker. The eastern extension also includes a plaque
recording Diana Princess of Wales (whose childhood home and burial place is at
nearby Althorp – *see* entry 9) being made a Freeman of the Borough in 1989; it
was unveiled by her brother, the 9th Earl Spencer, in 2002.

The building's façade features fourteen canopied statues, including monarchs
and famous people with close ties to the town. First-floor carvings illustrate
some of Aesop's fables, and below them are illustrations of Northampton life.
The arches of each ground floor window contain sculpted scenes of historical
events that took place in Northampton or the county.

In the modern courtyard is a statue of Northampton-born composer – and trumpeter – Malcolm Arnold.

Inside the Guildhall are a series of shields bearing the names and dates of every Mayor of Northampton since 1377 – 583 of them – forming a record seen hardly anywhere else in Britain.

30. Royal Theatre

This is another Grade II-listed Victorian gem, insignificant from the outside, but concealing a magnificent auditorium. It was designed by the renowned theatre architect Charles J. Phipps (responsible for forty theatres throughout Britain), and this 'charming Thespian temple', as it was described at the time, opened on 5 May 1884 with a production of *Twelfth Night*. Only three years later it was severely damaged by fire, but was restored and reopened.

The auditorium is built on three levels, with stalls and two horseshoe-shaped balconies supported by columns, and a single box on each side at Circle level. Many original features survive, including wooden benches in the Upper Circle, and a tiny box office on the original entrance stairs. The theatre's frontage bears the words 'Royal Theatre and Opera House'; apparently the words 'Theatre Royal' (as it was to have been known) were reversed by mistake, the change requiring special royal permission.

The theatre became home to the Northampton Repertory Players in 1927, and has been a 'producing house' (producing its own plays as well as hosting touring productions) ever since, with its own workshop and wardrobe department.

Above: The entrance to the 'Royal Theatre and Opera House'.

Right: The Royal's sumptuous Victorian auditorium, and Henry Bird's superb safety curtain. (Mike O'Dwyer)

Henry Irving's mulberry walking stick and other memorabilia displayed in the Royal's foyer.

Today it seats some 580 people, and is a rare surviving 'hemp house', with a 'fly gallery' from which scenery can be flown in and out by means of ropes. In 1933 a young Errol Flynn appeared here as part of the Rep Company before finding fame in Hollywood. Sir Henry Irving was one of many eminent theatrical figures to have performed here, and his walking stick, with Garrick associations, is in the foyer (*see* entry 31).

In 1960 the Royal was restored and redecorated, and was further overhauled in 1983, when the modern, larger Derngate auditorium was added next door on the site of the town's former bus station. Designed as a multi-purpose space, it can accommodate 1,200–1,400 people in a range of configurations.

In 1999 the two venues combined, run by the Northampton Theatres Trust, then in 2005 both closed for an 18-month, £14.5-million redevelopment and refurbishment, with the Royal returned to its original Victorian splendour. There was now a new main entrance, joint foyer and new performance and rehearsal spaces, and the complex reopened as Royal & Derngate in October 2006. In more recent years two luxurious, studio-style Errol Flynn Filmhouses have been opened on the site, making this award-winning venue one of the best arts complexes in the Midlands.

31. Abington Park

Mentioned in the Domesday Book, the village of Abington, now a Northampton suburb, once had a medieval manor house and mill, and was the site of gallows used to hang five suspected witches following trials in the town in 1612, thought to have been an early use of the ducking stool.

The house was once the home of Shakespeare's granddaughter Elizabeth Bernard. His last living descendent, she died in 1670 and is buried in the adjacent late twelfth-century church. The house then passed to the Thursby family and was enlarged and remodelled in the classical Georgian style. Anne Thursby was a lover of Shakespeare and close friend of renowned Shakespearean actor David Garrick, and in 1778 he planted a mulberry tree in the garden 'as a growing testament to their Friendship'. Legend has it that the tree was a cutting from one in Shakespeare's garden at New Place in Stratford-upon-Avon, reputedly given to him by King James I in 1608, the year Elizabeth was born. The ancient drooping tree can still be seen today.

Abington Park now houses museums dedicated to Northampton's history.

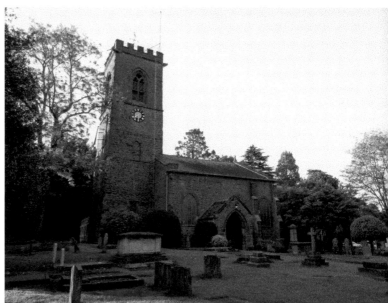

St Peter & St Paul, Abington, where Shakespeare's granddaughter Elizabeth Bernard is buried.

The new mulberry, planted by
Shakespearean actor Michael
Pennington on 23 April 2016.

In 1903 Sir Henry Irving visited Northampton to appear at the Royal Theatre
and was presented with a walking stick cut from Garrick's tree. In 1957 Irving's
grandson Lawrence presented the stick to the theatre, where it is on display
today (*see* entry 30).

In 1964 a second tree was planted by Sir Gyles Isham to mark
the 400th anniversary of the playwright's birth, then on 23 April 2016, the
400th anniversary of his death, a third mulberry was planted near the house
by renowned Shakespearean actor Michael Pennington (who was playing *King
Lear* at the Royal), thus perpetuating a unique tradition spanning almost two
and a half centuries.

In 1841 the manor was sold and the house became a lunatic asylum until
1892, following which the house and grounds were donated to Northampton by
Lady Wantage, opening in 1897 to celebrate Queen Victoria's Diamond Jubilee.
A museum was first established in 1899, then following complete restoration
the house was reopened in 1994, housing displays about the social and military
history of Northampton and the county, as well as a Museum of Leathercraft,
commemorating Northamptonshire's famous association with shoemaking.

The park itself is now a popular open space of some 120 acres, featuring
a bandstand, café and aviary. The remains of the former medieval village,
including two old gateposts, can still be seen within the grounds.

32. No. 78 Derngate

Just along the road from the Royal & Derngate is a small, unassuming-looking house that brings together the stories of two remarkable men: model-maker W. J. Bassett-Lowke and architect and designer Charles Rennie Mackintosh.

Wenman Joseph Bassett-Lowke (1877–1953), son of a Northampton boilermaker, took up the hobby of making model stationary steam engines, then, after visiting the Paris Exhibition in 1900, where he saw German model trains, he began manufacturing high-quality large- and small-scale models in Northampton, from 15-inch-gauge models to large tabletop systems. Among his many local interests he was a founder Director of the Northampton Repertory Theatre in 1926.

Glasgow-born Charles Rennie Mackintosh (1868–1928) was a leading architect of the 'Glasgow style', a movement related to Art Nouveau, and also designed the interiors, textiles, furniture and metalwork for his houses. He is mainly remembered for his work on the Glasgow School of Art.

A modest early nineteenth-century terraced house, No. 78 Derngate was bought for Bassett-Lowke as a wedding present by his father in 1916, and Wenman and his wife Florence lived there for ten years. Already keen on modern architecture and design, and the concepts of 'streamlining' and 'fitness for purpose', around this time Bassett-Lowke was introduced to Mackintosh, and commissioned him to transform the rather pokey and old-fashioned house into a modern and convenient home. An extension was added to the rear, enlarging the rooms on several floors and providing bedroom balconies. Inside, Mackintosh designed all the decoration, giving a remarkable and at times startling appearance to the small rooms.

In 1964 the house was bought by Northampton High School for Girls, and in 1968 was listed Grade II*. Let out as offices, then used as classrooms, it was feared locally that the character of the house might be lost unless it was preserved in some way. In the early 1990s the school sold it and, with encouragement from the Charles Rennie Mackintosh Society, it was acquired by Northampton Borough Council, together with No. 80 next door. A 78 Derngate Northampton Trust was formed and in 2001, with widespread financial support, the £1.4-million

The modest exterior of
No. 78 Derngate gives no clue to the
astonishing interior design.

Above left: Mackintosh design details on the staircase.

Above right: Somewhat startling styling in the guest bedroom!

restoration could begin. No. 78 was sensitively restored and the original 1916–19 scheme reinstated, while No. 80 was completely remodelled to become a new visitor centre and exhibition space showcasing the work of both the men who were instrumental in the creation of this significant and remarkable house.

33. National Lift Tower

At the other end of the architectural spectrum is this striking tower, built in 1980–82 by the Express Lift Company, which had manufactured lifts in Northampton since 1909 at the Abbey Works. After a long history, the company failed in 1997 and was taken over by Otis.

Dubbed locally the 'Northampton Lighthouse', and designed to test lifts and train lift engineers, the tower was commissioned in 1978, and was opened by the Queen in November 1982. It is 127.5 metres (418 feet) tall, and 14.6 metres (48 feet) in diameter at the base, tapering to 8.5 metres (28 feet) at the top. The surface of its sleek concrete casing is punctuated only by small windows, while its 'crenellated'

Above left: The former Express Lifts tower now stands incongruously within a modern housing estate.

Above right: The dizzying height of the 127.5-metre (418-foot) 'Northampton Lighthouse'.

top makes it somewhat reminiscent of Sauron's Dark Tower in *The Lord of the Rings*! It is the only lift-testing tower in Britain, and one of only two in Europe; it gained Grade II listing in 1997, becoming the youngest listed building in the UK.

With the takeover of Express by Otis, the tower fell out of use, and in 1999 it and the land surrounding it were sold for redevelopment. As a result, the tower now stands, rather incongruously, in the centre of a modern housing estate.

When the National Lift Partnership took over the tower it had almost no facilities, but following extensive renovation and repairs the newly renamed National Lift Tower reopened in October 2009. There are six lift shafts of varying heights and speeds, and several other vertical spaces, the tallest being 93 metres. The height of the tower and its unique features make it a valuable resource for testing height safety and access equipment and escape systems. It is also the world's tallest drainage testing facility.

The drop test shaft that was originally used to test lift safety equipment is 30 metres tall. A relatively weak section was built into the floor of the shaft with a gravel bed underneath, so that if an object should make an uncontrolled fall the foundations of the tower would not be damaged.

Abseiling is also popular for those with a head for heights! Commencing in 2011, the tower is the base for the National Abseil Centre, and at over 400 feet is the tallest permanent abseil tower in the world. The Borough Council allows it to be used up to twenty-four times a year for this purpose.

The County at War

34. Ashby St Ledgers: Birthplace of the Gunpowder Plot

Ashby St Ledgers, named from the village church dedicated to St Leodegarius, lies on the western edge of the county. In 1375 the manor passed to the Catesby family, but a century later it was confiscated and William Catesby executed following his support for King Richard III at the Battle of Bosworth. It was, however, regained by his son, but the family were staunchly Catholic, and suffered from fines and periodic imprisonment as a result.

The manor's central position made it a convenient meeting place when the Catholic conspirators were hatching the 'Gunpowder Plot' to blow up the Protestant King James I and his Parliament on 5 November 1605. At that time the house was owned by Robert Catesby's widowed mother; he lived at Chastleton in Oxfordshire but, being himself a recent widower, he visited often. As one of the prime movers of the conspiracy, tradition has it that he and his colleagues met in a room above the half-timbered gatehouse (now Grade II listed), away from the main house so as not to implicate his mother, and with a clear view of the surrounding area. Arms and munitions were amassed, Robert claiming that he was organising a regiment to fight in the Low Countries.

Beautiful Ashby St Ledgers, with the Edwin Lutyens extension on the left.

The Gunpowder Plotters are said to have met in the room above this gatehouse.

As is well known, the plot failed when one of the conspirators, Francis Tresham of Rushton Hall (*see* entry 15), warned his brother-in-law, Lord Monteagle, not to attend Parliament that day, and suspicions were aroused. Catesby fled direct from London to Holbeche House, Staffordshire (waving to his mother from the gate at Ashby as he passed, or so legend has it), where he was shot dead after a siege on the 8th.

As a result of Catesby's treachery, the manor was once more confiscated, then sold, passing through several owners before being acquired by Ivor Guest, 1st Baron Wimborne, in 1903. He employed the renowned architect Sir Edwin Lutyens to modify the manor and do some work in the village. Although sold between 1976 and 1998 (at one time being owned by the British Airways Pension Fund), the manor, though not the estate, was reacquired by the 3rd Viscount Wimborne, who undertook extensive restoration to save it from total ruin. Today this breathtakingly beautiful house, still in the possession of the Guest family, can be hired by private or corporate groups.

35. Naseby Battlefield

The Battle of Naseby was fought on the morning of 14 June 1645 and was the decisive action of the first English Civil War. Following a disappointing and indecisive performance by the Parliamentary army at Newbury at the end of 1644, Oliver Cromwell worked to improve the cohesion and professionalism of the formerly uncoordinated force by creating his 'New Model Army'.

The Royalists had taken Leicester, a Parliamentary stronghold, so the 'Roundheads', commanded by Oliver Cromwell and Sir Thomas Fairfax, hurried north from a siege of the Royalist base of Oxford. The King decided to give battle rather than be seen to be retreating north, but in open fields near the village of Naseby the engagement, lasting some three hours, resulted in the main Royalist field army being all but destroyed. Of 12,000 men, about 1,000 died, with 6,000 casualties, while the 15,000-strong New Model Army lost fewer than 150 men. All the Royalist artillery and stores were lost, and the King would never again be able to field an effective army.

The King's incriminating private papers were captured, revealing his attempts to draw foreign mercenaries into the war, thus strengthening the Parliamentary cause against him.

It is said that Naseby was the most important and decisive battle ever fought in England, setting the scene for significant political revolution and establishing Parliament's right to play a permanent role in the government of the kingdom. It also saw for the first time a well-organised, regular and uniformed force, and is seen by many as the birth of the modern British Army.

The battlefield itself, despite the addition of hedges and farm buildings, remains well preserved, although the incursion of the new A14 trunk road

The battlefield memorial at Naseby.

in 1992 caused considerable controversy and protest. The location is easily accessible, and the lie of the land over which the battle was fought and how the engagement unfolded can be readily appreciated from the battlefield memorial.

In January 2016 the Naseby Battlefield Project received Heritage Lottery funding to develop a new visitor centre as an information resource about the battle itself, the Civil War, the political and social history of the era and the rural environment of the 1600s, all of which will be a valuable addition to our understanding of this historic event.

36. Royal Military Depot, Weedon Bec

The French Revolution of 1789 posed a threat to the established European powers, and Britain and her allies were almost constantly at war with France during that period. The 1802 Treaty of Amiens brought a truce, but Napoleon's continued aggression meant that war resumed in May 1803.

Britain therefore made preparations for an expected invasion. The Grand Union Canal had arrived at Weedon, strategically located on Watling Street (and supposedly the furthest place in England from the sea), as recently as 1796, and an 1803 Act of Parliament authorised an area to be developed 'for the service of His Majesty's Ordnance'. The canal was an essential transport artery, and a short branch was cut to serve the depot, entering it beneath a lodge equipped with a moveable portcullis. When the London & Birmingham Railway followed in the late 1830s, it was also connected to the depot by a branch line.

The facility was the central small arms depot for the British Army. Largely built in 1805–06, it consisted of eight large two-storey buildings, 160 feet

The eight buildings of the Ordnance Depot flank the central canal basin.

The rear of the entrance lodge where road and canal entered.

The portcullis beneath the lodge. The link to the Grand Union canal has now disappeared.

long by 35 feet wide, each divided into four rooms. They flanked a central quarter-mile stretch of canal and were surrounded by a high stone wall. Small arms were stored in the upper floors, and larger items such as field artillery on the lower floors. In 1806 it was said to store sufficient to arm 200,000 men, together with 140 pieces of cannon.

Beyond, the canal passed through another lodge with a portcullis to enter a further walled and gated area, with four thick-walled gunpowder magazines separated by 'blast houses' filled with earth as a precaution against explosions. Remarkably, all these buildings survive today, and are listed Grade II*.

In the village there also used to be stables and barracks for 500 men, but these were demolished in the 1950s. Three spacious 'Pavilions' accommodated the principal officers, and here King George III would have lived had Napoleon successfully invaded.

The depot became redundant in 1965, and in 1984 was sold by the Ministry of Defence. The buildings are now used by light industry and shops (including an excellent second-hand bookshop) open to the public during normal hours and well worth a visit. In more recent years a volunteer group has been working to interpret the site's history and hopes to open a Heritage Lottery-funded visitor centre in the near future.

37. US Air Force Airfield Memorials

At the beginning of the Second World War there were few airfields in Northamptonshire, but by 1941 the RAF had a considerable presence. The United States Army Air Force (USAAF) arrived in 1942, and by 1944 there were eighteen air bases, seven being used by the USAAF, with almost 20,000 men. The Americans' contribution to ultimate victory is commemorated by several airfield memorials, four of which are featured here.

The first raid of the war by Eighth Air Force bombers took off from Grafton Underwood on 17 August 1942, and the last raid, against the tank factories in Pilsen, took off on 25 April 1945, after which the 384th Bomber Group (the airfield's longest resident) returned it to the RAF. In all, 316 missions were flown from here and more than 1,500 personnel were killed. The roadside memorial was unveiled in 1977, and there is a stained-glass window in the village church.

Construction of Kings Cliffe airfield started in 1942, and USAAF fighter units used 'Station 367' from 1943 until the end of the war. Because it was more than 50 miles west of any other fighter airfield, its operational capability was limited. Glenn Miller played his last airfield band concert here in October 1944, and a separate memorial commemorates the event. Post-war the airfield held German PoWs, then was an RAF ammunition store until sold off in January 1959.

The 384th Bombardment Group memorial at Grafton Underwood.

Left: The Polebrook 351st Bombardment Group memorial, with surviving airfield buildings evident.

Below: The Kings Cliffe Station 367 memorial, incorporating USAAF and RAF aircraft 'halves'.

The memorial to the airfield and its squadrons was unveiled by HRH the Duke of Gloucester in 1983.

Polebrook airfield was handed over to the Eighth Air Force in 1942, with accommodation for more than 2,000 personnel. The 97th Bomb Group was the first resident, followed by the 351st Bomb Group until the end of the war. In 1948 the airfield was declared inactive, but in 1959–63 became home to a Thor ballistic missile squadron. The 351st's most famous member was Hollywood actor Clark Gable, who flew several missions from Polebrook as an observer.

Harrington airfield was built by the USAAF in 1943/44, and was the furthest Eighth Air Force combat airfield from the east coast. The Americans left in July 1945, and the airfield was unused until it became another RAF Thor missile site. It is now home to the Harrington 'Carpetbaggers' aviation museum, with its comprehensive collections of wartime memorabilia. In 1987 a memorial was dedicated to the memory of those who did not survive the war. Located on the site of one of the former aircraft dispersal points, it depicts a 'Carpetbagger' B-24 Liberator taking off.

The main hall at the Harrington Aviation Museum.

County Communications

38. Watford Gap

Watford Gap is a name familiar to countless thousands of motorists, if only for the service area of that name on the M1 motorway. Hardly a 'gem', perhaps, but a crucial and fascinating geographical feature in the south-western half of the county nonetheless.

The 'gap' itself is barely discernible on the ground, but is a significant dip in the limestone hills that form the spine of Northamptonshire. A tributary of the River Nene rises at Watford village and flows east, while at Kilsby a tributary of the River Leam rises and flows west. This gap has, over two millennia, developed as a vitally important part of the North–South corridor, and at Watford the A5 road, railway, canal and motorway, reading west to east, are squeezed into an area only some 400 metres wide.

Though no doubt used long before they invaded, the Romans were first to leave their mark in the first century AD, with their road from London to Wroxeter, near Shrewsbury, known as Watling Street (later the A5 London–Holyhead trunk road). In coaching days it was an important north–south/east–west crossroads, and there was a coaching inn here known as 'The Watford Gap'.

Much later, in the early nineteenth century, the Leicester line of the Grand Union Canal was built, intertwining with Watling Street and climbing through Watford locks to a summit just beyond the gap, piercing the ridge by the 1,528-yard Crick Tunnel, completed in 1814.

Just over twenty years later Robert Stephenson chose the gap for his London & Birmingham Railway, opened in stages in 1837–38. The line climbs continually from Weedon to a summit at the south end of the 1 mile 666 yards of Kilsby Tunnel (*see* entry 41), which too pierces the ridge; the line then drops all the way to Rugby.

On 2 November 1959 the M1 motorway arrived, and on that day Watford Gap services opened, making them the oldest motorway services in Britain. They were originally managed by Blue Boar, a company that owned several petrol

Above left: Watford Gap services on the M1, looking south.

Above right: Looking from the canal bridge, with Watling Street behind the camera, the railway and motorway bridges can be seen.

stations in the area, including one with a café on the A5 near Watford; they were invited to run the services as compensation for loss of trade. The services became famous and had a long, colourful and chequered history. Roadchef purchased the facility from Blue Boar in 1995, and the 50th anniversary was celebrated in November 2009, with various events including a musical about the services!

39. Stoke Bruerne and The Canal Museum

The Grand Junction Canal (later part of the Grand Union Canal) opened between London and Braunston in Northamptonshire in 1800, except for the tunnel at Blisworth, which took a few more years to complete (*see* entry 40). The canal headed north into the county through what would much later become Milton Keynes, using the valley of the River Tove, and eventually climbing out of that valley by a series of locks to reach Stoke Bruerne.

Alongside the top lock are a colourful collection of shops and cafés, both floating and land-based, and two canal-side pubs. Here also is The Canal Museum, established in 1963 and formerly known as the National Waterways Museum, gaining its present title when the Canal & River Trust was established in 2010. It is housed in two storeys of a restored corn mill.

Designated of national importance by the Arts Council, the Trust's museum collection is housed here as well as sites at Ellesmere Port, Gloucester, the Anderton Boat Lift and Standedge Visitor Centre. Providing an excellent overview of the history of Britain's inland waterways, The Canal Museum tells the story of the canals, the engineers and navvies who built them, and the people who worked on them.

Above: A busy Bank Holiday scene at Stoke Bruerne as a boat descends through the lock.

Left: The fascinating Canal Museum is housed in a restored corn mill.

Exhibits include a recreation of a boat-builder's workshop with its specialist tools, displays of traditional clothing and boaters' painted crafts and belongings, historical signs and notices, and working models of historic boats of all kinds. In addition, films and videos bring the historic exhibits to life. An audio guide is free with museum entry. Altogether, the Trust's collection consists of more than 12,000 objects including sixty-eight historic boats and the extensive National Waterways archive.

Outside the museum is moored the narrowboat *Sculptor*, and an easy walk along the well-surfaced towpath brings the visitor to the southern portal of Blisworth Tunnel.

40. Blisworth Tunnel

Blisworth Tunnel cuts through Blisworth Hill between Stoke Bruerne and Blisworth. At 3,076 yards (2,813 metres) long, it is the third longest navigable canal tunnel in Britain – only Standedge in West Yorkshire and Dudley in the West Midlands are longer. Blisworth is also the ninth longest canal tunnel in the world. At its deepest point it is about 143 feet below ground level. It is also the widest freely navigable tunnel in Europe (at water level it is 5 metres wide, sufficient for two narrowboats to pass).

Remarkably, having been excavated with nothing more than picks, shovels and wheelbarrows, the tunnel is very nearly dead straight, although an error left a 'wiggle' of more than a metre in the centre.

A narrowboat enters the south portal of Blisworth Tunnel past the blacksmith's forge. The Transport Trust's 'Red Wheel' award plaque is affixed to the wall.

Work began in 1793, but after three years the tunnel collapsed due to quicksand; fourteen men lost their lives. A new tunnel was begun on a different alignment, by which time almost the whole of the rest of the Grand Junction Canal had been completed. While the tunnel was dug, in 1801 a temporary horse-drawn double-track tramway was laid over the top of the hill (becoming Northamptonshire's first railway). Finally, in March 1805 the tunnel was completed.

Because there was no towpath in the tunnel, initially boats were 'legged' through, whereby men ('leggers') lay on their backs and 'walked' the boat through using their feet against the tunnel walls. In 1871 steam tugs were introduced to take boats back and forth, and extra ventilation shafts were dug. The tugs were in use until 1936, by which time motor boats, towing a 'butty boat', became the norm.

By the late 1970s the tunnel was becoming increasingly unnavigable after failures in the brick lining, and in 1982–84 a major rebuilding project was undertaken, lining the tunnel with pre-cast 6.5-metre-diameter concrete rings (trying out materials and techniques that were later used in the Channel Tunnel). One of the rings is displayed near the tunnel's south portal. The tunnel was pumped dry and converted to a road tunnel so that lorries could bring in materials; but the drivers had to become accustomed to reversing for half a mile!

In 2014, the 30th anniversary of the reopening, the tunnel was awarded a Transport Trust 'Red Wheel' to recognise its industrial heritage and importance; the plaque is affixed to the blacksmith's forge at the south portal, a designated a Grade II-listed structure.

41. Kilsby Tunnel

Kilsby Tunnel, on today's West Coast Main Line, was built for the London & Birmingham Railway, engineered by Robert Stephenson. Although at the time the longest tunnel ever attempted for steam locomotives, at 2,426 yards long, it is only the eighteenth longest in Britain. However, its construction was an epic of engineering endeavour.

Tradition, since denied, has it that the people of Northampton wanted nothing to do with the railway, so the line bypassed the town to the west, having to negotiate the high ground between Weedon and Rugby. Begun in May 1835, the tunnel took much longer and cost much more than anticipated as a result of quicksand, which caused flooding and a roof collapse in 1836. The original contractor fell ill and died, and the Stephensons took over, working with direct labour. To rescue the project thirteen steam pumps were used, lifting up to 2,000 gallons a minute, but it took nineteen months to bring the water under control. In March 1838, 70 yards of tunnel collapsed and had to be repaired. In the end it took three years and cost around £300,000, three times the original estimate. Meanwhile travellers on the remainder of the line had to travel by stagecoach between Denbigh Hall, north of Bletchley, and Rugby to continue their journey by train. A maximum of 1,200 men and 200 horses were employed, and twenty-six men lost their lives.

The tunnel was dug from twenty-five working shafts, and to allay early travellers' fears of suffocation it was designed to be unusually high at 28 feet. Nine of the working shafts were retained for ventilation. The smaller ones are brick chimneys 9 feet in diameter, but two of them were opened out to a diameter of 60 feet, topped by distinctive castellated towers and between 100 and 130 feet deep; they are now listed structures. The southern one can clearly be seen from the M45 motorway, while the other stands adjacent to the A5.

It is said that some 30 million bricks were used in the tunnel's construction, and the sturdy tunnel portals (Grade II* listed in 1987) are of stone with projecting parapets.

Sadly, the south portal can no longer be seen from the road, but this 1982 view shows an electric unit heading southwards. (I. Worland, Colour-Rail)

One of the two great castellated ventilation shafts stands beside the A5; a smaller one is visible in the distance.

On 23 December 1837 the Stephensons and their engineers enjoyed a gala dinner at the Dun Cow Inn at Dunchurch to celebrate completion of the tunnel. Public services began on 17 September 1838, and the tunnel has remained in use ever since.

42. Harringworth (Welland) Viaduct

Harringworth Viaduct, sometimes called the Welland Viaduct, was built by the Midland Railway over the broad valley of the River Welland between March 1876 and July 1878. It carries the railway between Corby in Northamptonshire and Manton Junction in Rutland; at Manton the line joined the existing MR Peterborough-Stamford-Melton Mowbray line. The viaduct is some 60–70 feet high and 1,275 yards long with eighty-two arches each of 40-foot span, making it the longest masonry viaduct in Britain. Every ninth pier is a 'king' pier with a pilaster (these isolate the piers in sets and prevent any strains being continued indefinitely from arch to arch). There is a corbelled-out track-worker's refuge at every fourth pier.

The red bricks for the viaduct were made and fired onsite using local clay deposits; a contemporary newspaper account states that 26,000,000 were used. Some bear children's fingerprints and footprints, suggesting that child labour may have been used in their making – or they may simply have walked on the clay-filled moulds before firing! Over the years the viaduct's size, age and exposure to the elements has led to some deterioration, and in more recent years some areas of brickwork have been replaced by predominantly blue engineering bricks, which are more water-resistant and stronger, giving today's structure a somewhat patchwork appearance.

Goods trains began to use the viaduct on 6 December 1879, with passenger traffic following in March 1880. By that time the Midland's main line between

Above: It is almost impossible to capture the 1,275 yards of the viaduct in a single picture.

Left: The mighty viaduct is between 60 and 70 feet high.

London St Pancras and Glendon South Junction, just north of Kettering, had been quadrupled, giving two tracks in each direction; the new goods lines were especially valuable in handling the relatively slow-moving coal trains from the Midlands to London. The new line to Manton and beyond effectively extended this quadrupling from Glendon to Nottingham and Leicester, giving the Midland a new main line to the north.

Regular passenger services were withdrawn in 1967, and today the viaduct carries very little passenger traffic, although in 2009 a single daily passenger service was introduced between Melton Mowbray and St Pancras via Corby, the first regular passenger service to use the viaduct since the 1960s. The line is mostly used by freight and as a diversionary route, although the occasional steam-hauled special uses the line, and is much photographed while crossing this impressive Grade II-listed structure.

43. Roade Cutting

Yet another example of railway engineering achievement can be seen just north of Roade on the West Coast Main Line. Completed in 1838 and some 1½ miles long and 65 feet deep, Roade Cutting proved to be the most troublesome earthwork on the London & Birmingham Railway. The contractor had to deal with unstable ground, springs and crumbling rock, similar to conditions experienced at Blisworth canal tunnel (*see* entry 40), only a mile or so to the east. Pumping engines had to be installed, and walls built to underpin the rock. As at

A northbound electric train passes the lower-level Northampton line in Roade Cutting.

Kilsby Tunnel (*see* entry 41), the contractor failed, and Robert Stephenson had to take over the works. So narrow was the cutting that only a limited number of men could work in it, which further hampered progress. In the end, with the sole exception of Kilsby Tunnel, the cutting was the last work on the L&BR to be completed.

When the line was quadrupled in 1880–81, the east side of the cutting was widened to take the extra tracks, which formed the southern end of the Northampton loop. This latter line entered the cutting at a lower level, so the cutting had to be further deepened to allow the new tracks to climb towards Roade station. A landslide closed the Northampton line in 1890, when heavy rain caused the weak clay and limestone layers beneath to give way. The low-level line was subsequently protected by heavy retaining walls braced with overhead iron girders, which can still be seen today from the various roads and footbridges.

An interesting outcome of this great engineering endeavour is that today the cutting is designated by Natural England as a geological Site of Special Scientific Interest. As Natural England points out, 'rail cuttings form a very important part of the geological resource of England... [Many] are in areas where natural geological exposures are rare or absent [and they] provide much better exposure of geological features than comparable natural exposures.' The designated 15-hectare site, from the site of Roade station to the north end of the cutting where the Rugby and Northampton lines diverge, exposes rock formations that are between 168.3 and 167.1 million years old. This listing will ensure that the cutting is protected against anything that might harm its special features, together with management of vegetation.

So Roade Cutting has considerable scientific importance besides being a great place to watch trains!

44. Brampton Valley Way and the Northampton & Lamport Railway

The London & North Western Railway's Northampton to Market Harborough line opened in February 1859, and passenger services were withdrawn just over a century later in 1960. Despite a couple of reinstatements, the line closed for good in 1981, and eventually the track was lifted. However, in 1987 a 14-mile (22km) section was purchased by Northamptonshire County Council with grant aid from the Countryside Commission, and was redeveloped as a linear park, one of the longest in the country to use a railway trackbed.

The route from Boughton Crossing, north of Northampton, to Little Bowden Crossing, just south of Market Harborough, opened in 1993 and is deservedly popular with walkers and cyclists; it forms an off-road section of the Sustrans National Cycle Network. Horse-riding is permitted on certain sections (contact the rangers for more details), while nearby there are shops and pubs in Brixworth village (famous for its Saxon church – *see* entry 23), and pubs in Maidwell and Oxendon. The surface is rolled stone, making for easy going. There is free car parking at various locations along the way, and guided walks and cycle rides.

What makes the path unusual is that there are two former railway tunnels to negotiate. Originally twin-bore tunnels, one bore remains passable in each case, at Kelmarsh (322 yards/294 metres) and Oxendon (462 yards/422 metres). They are unlit, but fun and exciting to travel through! Alternative routes over the tunnels are provided for the less intrepid.

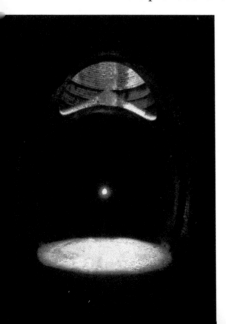

Walking or cycling through Oxendon Tunnel is an exciting experience.

A section of the Brampton Valley Way runs alongside the Northampton & Lamport Railway, a rebuilt heritage line based on the site of the former Pitsford & Brampton station, which closed in 1950. In 1984 enthusiasts began to rebuild the line and reinstate a station, which now boasts a buffet, gift shop and second-hand bookshop. The booking office is the top half of Lamport signal box, and the new signal box is from Little Bowden Crossing, near Market Harborough, and controls a full range of operational signals. By 1995 passenger trains were being run, and the railway was officially opened the following year. Since then the track has been extended both north and south of the station, affording a pleasant 1½-mile journey through beautiful rolling countryside behind heritage steam or diesel engines during the operating season from March to October.

The Northampton & Lamport Railway's rebuilt Pitsford & Brampton station.

Cyclists on the Brampton Valley Way stop to admire ex-GWR loco No. 1450 on the adjacent N&LR.

Racing and Recreation

45. Silverstone Circuit

The world-famous Silverstone motor-racing circuit is always thought of as being a Northamptonshire venue, but in fact half of this former RAF bomber station is in Buckinghamshire. It opened as an Operational Training Unit in 1943, with Wellington bombers. After the war it was vacated, and sold in 1947. That year an informal motor race was held on the deserted field, then in 1948 the RAC took a short lease and it was converted for use as a racing circuit, initially using the runways, then the fast perimeter tracks. In October 1948 it hosted the first British Grand Prix, watched by a crowd of 100,000. Hay bales and ropes protected the piggery and crops in the middle of the circuit!

In 1950 the race became the first in the newly created Formula 1 World Championship. The following year the British Racing Drivers' Club (BRDC) took over the RAC's lease and set about changing the airfield track into something more permanent, with better facilities for spectators.

From 1955 the race rotated between Silverstone, Aintree and Brands Hatch, but became a permanent resident at Silverstone in 1987, where the wide open spaces were better suited to the growing demand for more run-off areas.

Large-scale renovation in the 1990s saw the circuit changed considerably to reduce speed and increase driver safety. However, Silverstone's place as the home of the British Grand Prix was beginning to be called into doubt; in 2010 the race was set to move to Donington Park, but happily this fell through and a

The excitement of Formula 1: the start of the 2017 British Grand Prix. (Silverstone Circuit)

Lewis Hamilton passes 'The Wing' at Silverstone at the 2017 event. (Silverstone Circuit)

new long-term contract was negotiated. A new infield section was constructed, suitable for Moto GP motorcycle races, and a brand-new pit complex – dubbed 'The Wing' – was constructed.

Sadly, the economics of international motor racing led to an announcement in July 2017 that the BRDC was discontinuing its contract with Formula 1 owners Liberty Media. Considerable losses were being made, which meant that, unless a new arrangement could be reached, 2019 would be the last year that the British Grand Prix would take place at Silverstone. However, it is the only venue currently licensed to run a Grand Prix in Great Britain, so all parties, including the 350,000 fans who attend, and the worldwide TV audience of 400 million, hope that a long-term financially viable solution can be found. A British GP away from Silverstone would be unthinkable!

46. Wicksteed Park

Wicksteed Park at Kettering is the second oldest theme park in the UK after Blackgang Chine on the Isle of Wight. It was founded by Leeds-born Charles Wicksteed (1847–1931), who spent some time with locomotive-builder Kitson & Co. before setting up his own engineering business in Kettering in 1876. In 1913 he purchased an area of meadowland with the intention of developing a village for the working classes at below-average rents, offering generous gardens and a large open public space for recreation; plans dated 1914 describe a 'Barton Seagrave Garden Suburb Estate', but it did not come to fruition.

It is said that, to celebrate the end of the First World War, Wicksteed's factory built some children's swings from central heating pipes removed from the works, creating the first commercial playground. Such was its success that Wicksteed's company became the world's first playground manufacturing company, and is still operating. In 1917 the first playground equipment was installed, designed and built by Wicksteed's engineering company.

The full 147-acre park opened in 1921, and soon crowds were arriving by road and rail. Today it is still a hugely popular family day out with a wide variety of entertainments grouped around a playground, a fairground, the 12-hectare lake fed by the River Ise, and the arena, which contains the park's larger rides. Open all year round, the playground is said to be the largest free facility of its kind in Europe.

In 1922–23 a Pavilion and Theatre were added, subsequently enlarged and now used for a variety of events, including weddings. This building was followed in 1924 by an adjacent terraced Rose Garden.

One of the attractions is the Water Chute, dating from 1926 and fully renovated in 2002; it is the oldest working ride in the UK. There is also a

Traditional entertainment at the fairground area at Wicksteed Park.

The 1920s Pavilion overlooks the peaceful terraced gardens.

Locomotive *Merlin* heads a train on the Wicksteed Park Railway around the lake.

2-foot-gauge railway running round the lake; opened in 1931, it is estimated that more than 15 million people have ridden on it. It was the last feature of the park to be added during Wicksteed's lifetime, and today is supported by the Friends of the Wicksteed Park Railway.

The park is now owned by the Wicksteed Charitable Trust, set up by Wicksteed himself as the Wicksteed Village Trust in 1916, and offers education as well as entertainment, with various study programmes available for schools.

47. Brixworth and Sywell Country Parks

Northamptonshire has half a dozen country parks and more than eighty pocket parks. The 'gems' that have been chosen to represent them are two that are based around reservoirs.

Pitsford Water is a 413-hectare reservoir, the largest body of water in the county. It was built in 1956 to supply drinking water to Northampton, about 6 miles away. Owner Anglian Water manages the reservoir as a water park for walking, cycling, fishing, sailing and birdwatching. A causeway crosses the northern part, and beyond that is the Pitsford Water Nature Reserve, managed by the Wildlife Trust for Bedfordshire, Cambridgeshire and Northamptonshire. Four streams feed the reservoir at this upper end, and their valleys form large bays of shallow water that are excellent feeding and sheltering areas for wintering wildfowl – up to 10,000 birds. More than sixty species of birds breed on the site in spring and summer. A well-marked hard-surfaced 7-mile trail winds around the water, through woodlands and meadows, affording extensive views.

Paddleboarding is one many water sports to be enjoyed at Pitsford reservoir.

Six swans a-swimming ... extensive sailing and fishing facilities are also available.

The reservoir was designated a biological Site of Special Scientific Interest (SSSI) in 1970.

Also sharing the site is Brixworth Country Park. Opened in 1997, it includes cycle hire and a caféteria, and is run by Northamptonshire County Council. The park boasts a network of accessible surfaced trails around the reservoir, a sensory garden, and plenty of facilities for families, picnickers, walkers and cyclists.

Between Northampton and Wellingborough, near Earls Barton, is Sywell Country Park, also centred on a reservoir, built at the turn of the last century to supply water to the Higham Ferrers and Rushden areas. It operated from 1906 to 1979 and, like Pitsford, has been designated an SSSI. Today's park offers refreshment facilities, and the original Edwardian pump house buildings and valve tower are accompanied by a small arboretum and gardens laid out below the dam. The area known as the Filter Bed features sculptures and unusual sand and water play equipment as well as swings, slides and a play ship. For walkers

The Edwardian dam at Sywell Country Park.

Below the dam at Sywell are attractive gardens and play areas.

and cyclists, there are accessible trails stretching for 3 miles round the water. A waterworks heritage trail guide is available.

The reservoir is also a nationally renowned coarse fishery, famous in particular for its tench, which grow to more than 10lb.

As can be appreciated, both country parks offer a broad range of recreational opportunities, and both offer enjoyable and rewarding days out for all the family.

48. Fineshade Wood

This large wooded area is located in the top corner of the county, and is managed by the Forestry Commission. It is part of the former royal hunting forest of Rockingham Forest (*see* entry 5). The visitor centre is at Top Lodge, off the A43 Corby–Stamford road, and includes a visitor centre, café and cycle

Above: Plenty of activities are available in Fineshade Wood for exercise and exploration ...

Left: ... but its tranquillity can also be enjoyed.

hire facility; the centre is environmentally friendly with solar panels, rainwater harvesting (for the toilets) and a reedbed sewerage system.

The wood takes its name from the former Fineshade Abbey; there was never a village here. The Forestry Commission describes it as

> an ancient mixed broadleaf and conifer woodland with waymarked walks, car park and Caravan Club site. The wood contains rich semi-natural native woodland, as well as areas of conifers that are gradually being restored to site-native broadleaf woodland under the 'Ancient Woodland Project'. The wood was coppiced for many centuries, and the remnant coppice banks can still be seen. The coppice was used in the past for charcoal-making, and there is evidence of medieval and Roman iron smelting in the wood.

Fineshade is also known for its population of red kites, which are becoming an increasingly common site throughout the county. Once on the brink of extinction, their reintroduction is one of the greatest British conservation success stories. In 1989 an official reintroduction programme was established in England and Scotland and the initial release of breeding pairs in the Chilterns led to the release of red kites at Rockingham Forest in the mid-1990s. Their numbers continue to expand, and Northamptonshire is one of the best places to see them.

Fineshade also has a regionally important population of adders and other reptiles as well as scarce breeding birds; dormice have recently been recorded together with great crested and palmate newts.

In 2015 a planning application to build holiday cabins in part of the publicly owned wood was rejected as potentially damaging to its biodiversity and character. The following year Fineshade was protected by a new local planning policy, which placed it within an 'Area of Tranquillity'.

There's plenty to do in the wood, besides enjoying its tranquillity. For example, there is currently a Gruffalo Spotters' trail supported by an 'augmented reality' app. Along the trail are clues that lead to marker posts, where Gruffalo characters Mouse, Fox, Owl, Snake and the Gruffalo itself appear.

49. The Jurassic Way

If you had the inclination and stamina, walking the Jurassic Way would be an ideal way to view many of the 'gems' featured in this book! This long-distance recreational walking route traverses Northamptonshire, linking two ancient market towns – Banbury in Oxfordshire and Stamford in Lincolnshire. It follows a band of Jurassic limestone – about 140–195 million years old – that runs along

A slightly drunken footpath sign indicates the Jurassic Way in Rockingham village.

the northern boundary of the county. It is identified by signposts, waymarkers and stiles and gates that carry the distinctive Jurassic Way logo – a fossil known as Kallirhynchia sharpi, one of many associated with nineteenth-century Northampton collector Samuel Sharp.

The trail is 88 miles (142 km) long, most of which is in Northamptonshire. It enters the county across the River Cherwell and passes through or near Charwelton, Fawsley and Ashby St Ledgers. The central section stretches from the Roman Watling Street near Watford Gap to the scarp of the Welland Valley, passing Sibbertoft and Sulby (villages on the fringes of Naseby battlefield), before crossing the Brampton Valley Way at Oxendon Tunnel. It passes through Rockingham village, under Harringworth Viaduct and past Fineshade Woods – all featured herein. This middle section includes some of the finest views in Northamptonshire. The northern section traverses the ancient Rockingham Forest, following closely the course of the River Welland before passing into Lincolnshire.

The route also crosses the course of the former Great Central Railway at Catesby and Woodford Halse – this was another late, great railway engineering achievement, which almost qualifies as a 'gem' itself. Other transport associations are a stretch along the Oxford Canal from Banbury and another waterside stretch along the Grand Union Canal near Braunston.

Detailed maps and guides courtesy of Northamptonshire County Council can be downloaded from the Internet, so why not lace up your walking boots and give it a try!

50. The Nene Way

Having travelled the length of the county from south-west to north-east by the Jurassic Way, this long-distance footpath crosses roughly west to east following the course of the River Nene. Incidentally, the pronunciation of the river's name is a source of uncertainty, and seems to depend on locality, but currently is it generally thought to be the 'Nenn' above Thrapston, and the 'Neen' below it!

The Nene is one of Northamptonshire's principal rivers, and the tenth longest in the UK, only 9 miles shorter than the Clyde, but less than half the length of the Thames. It rises in the county, its principal source being Arbury Hill, near

The Nene Way is clearly waymarked along the route.

Badby, although other small tributaries soon join it. From there it flows for 100 miles via Cambridgeshire and Norfolk to The Wash in Lincolnshire (about 50 miles within Northamptonshire), and an amazing 88 miles of that total length, from Northampton to the sea, are navigable. The river falls a total of 300 feet (91 metres) in its first 17 miles to the county town, but less than 200 feet (61 metres) from there to the sea. It has a catchment area of 631 square miles (1,630 sq. km).

In Northamptonshire the river meanders through typical rolling farmland as well as passing through the industrial areas around Northampton and Wellingborough, before passing into Cambridgeshire at Wansford, west of Peterborough. It has connections with the Grand Union Canal and the River Great Ouse.

Like the Jurassic Way, the Nene Way takes the walker past many of the places visited in this book. It connects with the Knightley Way (of Fawsley fame) and the Lyveden Way. Although it doesn't hug the riverbank, the path's meanderings take in through bluebell woods, wildlife havens, quiet countryside and some of the county's most picturesque villages, many with pubs and cafés. En route is takes in Thrapston, Oundle and Fotheringhay before reaching the county boundary near Wansford.

As with the Jurassic Way, guides to the path in Northamptonshire are available online, and divide the route in three sections, so shorter as well as longer walks are possible, depending on taste and ability!

The Nene Way passes close to the attractive riverside village of Denford, near Thrapston.

About the Author

Although born in London, Will Adams was brought up in Coventry, living there until he left to read English at Cambridge University. There he was a member of the well-known Footlights Club, but, failing to subsequently pursue a successful career as a scriptwriter and comedy actor, he moved into publishing via ladies' knitwear and crossword puzzles (long story). He was Senior Editor with transport publisher Patrick Stephens Limited (PSL), part of Thorsons, until going freelance in 1990. Today he divides his time between professional puzzle compiling, freelance book editing, and writing, including several railway books. Twenty years ago he returned to his earlier love of comedy by co-writing and appearing in annual plays, revues and pantomimes for the local drama group, as well as being one half of comic song duo 'Sweet F.A.'.

He is married to Tricia, a professional librarian, and has two daughters, one a musician and singer, the other a film producer.

Bibliography

Many websites have been consulted in the preparation of this book, especially the official sites of the locations concerned, and I would like to acknowledge the research and scholarship that has gone into them. Another useful site was that of Historic England (www.historicengland.org.uk).

The following books have also been consulted:

Adams, Will, *British Railways Past and Present: Northamptonshire* (2 vols, Past & Present Publishing, 2012 and 2013)

Biddle, Gordon, *Britain's Historic Railway Buildings* (Ian Allan 2011)

Billing, Chris, *Northamptonshire Curiosities* (Dovecote Press, 1993)

Bowyer, Michael J. F., *Action Stations: Vol. 6, Military Airfields of the Cotswolds and the Central Midlands* (Patrick Stephens Ltd, 1983)

Dry, Wakeling, *Northamptonshire* (Methuen, 2nd ed., 1914)

Howell, Michael and Ford, Peter, *The True History of the Elephant Man* (Penguin, 1980)

Mee, Arthur (ed.), *The King's England: Northamptonshire* (Hodder & Stoughton, 1946)

Northamptonshire Federation of Women's Institutes, *The Northamptonshire Village Book* (NFWI/Countryside Books, 1989)

Pevsner, Nikolaus, *The Buildings of England: Northamptonshire* (Yale University Press, revised ed., 1973)

Rolt, L. T. C., *George and Robert Stephenson* (Longman, 1960)